FISH
FOR YOU

FISH FOR YOU

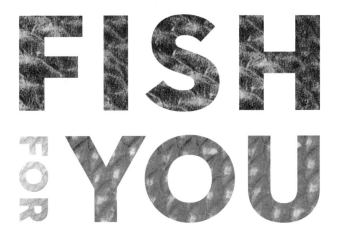

INSPIRED SEAFOOD
RECIPES FROM MARKET
TO PLATE

— CHEF —

SPENCER
WATTS

whitecap

EDITOR Penny Hozy
PROOFREADER Patrick Geraghty
DESIGNER Andrew Bagatella
FOOD PHOTOGRAPHY AND BEHIND THE SCENES IMAGES Steph Brown
COVER ART & ON LOCATION PHOTOGRAPHY Laine Mostert
SPENCER "AT HOME" PHOTOGRAPHY Roselyne Rheaume
ILLUSTRATIONS Eimear Kinsella

Library and Archives Canada Cataloguing in Publication

Watts, Spencer, author.
Fish for you / Spencer Watts.
Includes index.   ISBN: 978-1-77050-364-9 (softcover)
1. Cooking (Seafood)   2. Cooking (Fish)   3. Cookbooks
TX747 .W38 2021   641.6/92—dc23

Whitecap Books acknowledges the financial support of the Government of Canada
through the Canada Book Fund (CBF) for our publishing activities and the Province of
British Columbia through the Book Publishing Tax Credit.

Printed in Canada

whitecap.ca

Every story has a beginning and my story with fish and seafood starts with my parents. This book is dedicated to where it all started, long weekends on the boat. Thank you for submerging me in the magnificent beauty and culture of fishing, family, food, and stories.

CONTENTS

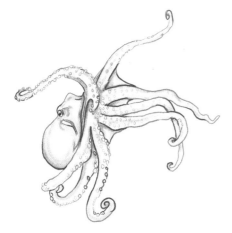
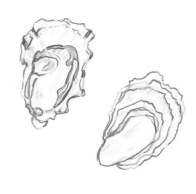

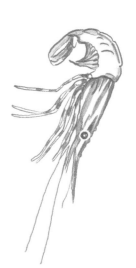

INTRODUCTION

Before I was the James Beard Award–winning host of a television series celebrating fish and seafood, I was the son of a sailor. I was born on the West Coast of British Columbia, and since I was a young lad I have always been on the water with a fishing rod in my hands. When I graduated from culinary school at the Pacific Institute of Culinary Arts in 2001, the first thing I did to celebrate was head up to our family cabin to go fishing.

This cookbook is full of memories, stories, experiences, and great food; whether it's a simple dinner for family and friends or a special dish for a dinner party, this book has something for every occasion. It's fun, tasty, and I hope you can make some of these dishes your new signatures.

I have cooked and eaten fish around the world and back, and along the way I have saved memories and been inspired by worldly flavours. This collection of recipes is for everyone, and I welcome you to the adventure of *Fish for You.*

Throughout my culinary career, fish has always been something I have gravitated towards. Is it all the experiences I had as a kid? The quality of local fish that I grew up around? Maybe it's both, or maybe it's because fish is simply amazing. It's delicate, has a limited peak freshness, takes on flavour while having a flavour of its own, and every time I cook it seems like a celebration. Whether it's scallops on fine china or a pasta loaded with prawns, for me, fish and seafood have that certain *je ne sais quoi.*

Some of my best memories are of being on the water, fishing. So much of who I am is because of my time with mother ocean, from searching out oyster beds on the Sunshine Coast to cold weather spot prawn season and fishing for salmon, cod, and even octopus in every imaginable weather pattern. Learning how to open oysters with my dad, or my mom teaching me how to clean fresh crab I had just caught, it has all been one great journey for me. This cookbook is a piece of every one of those unforgettable adventures paired with my love for cooking. It's a different look at fish and seafood, with new things to learn and a ton of inspiration for your next cooking adventure.

There have been so many teachers in my life when it comes to seafood and cuisine. I have learned from the best fishmongers, culinary seafood icons, and chefs over the years. To say this book is diverse is an understatement.

The culinary force behind this cookbook is all of these experiences. I can honestly say I am not a chef with a deep-rooted singular culinary style or vision; I'm a culinary globetrotter, and I say that with pride. When a dish has Japanese roots, it's because I have spent years examining its ingredients working alongside Japanese cooks and learning and making mistakes, going home after 12-hour shifts to practice what I had learned until it became an extension of my soul.

I love the spices and warmth of Indian cooking, and this has come with great mentorship from Chef Rajeev Aurora, who I worked with in my hotel days. I would come in on my days off and he would teach me how to use spices and make simple (and some not-so-simple) curries. This was another great obsession of mine, and still is.

My culinary training is French-based and there is a lot of that training in this book, from Chef Pascal teaching me how to make an authentic bouillabaisse, to Chef Robert Clark teaching me how to make the perfect bisque. I would have to say that my foundation of French technique–based cooking is one of my staples.

Eating dim sum at two years of age will definitely have an effect on someone who becomes a chef, and it did. Chinese cooking has had a deep impact on my culinary style and I love how those ingredients can rock your taste buds and add so much adventure to food, especially fish.

On one hand, fish and big bold flavours are really exciting, but so is a delicate approach. Working in an Italian restaurant was another huge culinary leap for me, using light sauces, fresh herbs, and the simple approach of Mediterranean cooking, which is perfect for fish. If you break fresh ingredients down to their core they can shine as bright as the sun, an approach that will always have a place in my heart and in this cookbook.

As a cook with over 20 years' experience I have fallen in love with so many cooking styles, and they all have a presence in this book—from Tex-Mex and cooking with my family in the States, to Spanish spices from working with Chef David Foot. This cookbook has it all and is unapologetically me to the core. I have taken all of my experiences and simmered them into a collection of fun, approachable recipes you can do at home. I hope this book inspires you to get some fish and get into the kitchen. Happy cooking!

CHAPTER NO. 1

HAPPY HOUR & OYSTERS

A good happy hour with oysters might be one of my favourite seafood experiences.
In this section, I've written some really fun happy hour dishes, cold fish preparations,
and my favourite raw and cooked oyster recipes.

CITRUS-MARINATED SCALLOP CEVICHE TOSTADA 6
with Chipotle Oil

SMOKED SALMON FLATBREAD 11
*with Crispy Roasted Chickpeas / Quick Pickled Red Onion /
Tikka Masala Cream Cheese / Tamarind Drizzle*

BRIOCHE SHRIMP TOAST 14
with Five-Spice Sweet and Sour Dip / Ginger Marmalade

DUNGENESS CRAB FRITTERS 19
with Spicy Red Pepper Relish / Lemon Yogurt

SPICY "CRUNCH ROLL" ALBACORE TUNA POKE 22
*with Teriyaki Glaze / Crunchy Tempura Flakes /
Spicy Sriracha Mayo / Avocado–Mango Salsa*

BLACKENED AHI TUNA TATAKI 27
with Red Slaw / Creole Mustard Vinaigrette

BAKED MUSSELS ON THE HALF SHELL 30
with Chipotle Butter / Herbed Breadcrumbs

FRESH SHUCKED OYSTERS 35
with Rosé Mignonette / Wasabi–Maple Vinaigrette / Seafood Sauce

CORNMEAL FRIED POPCORN OYSTERS 38
with Horse-Ranchish Dipping Sauce

OVEN-BROILED SWEET MISO OYSTERS 43
with Sautéed Spinach / Chili Breadcrumbs

CITRUS-MARINATED SCALLOP CEVICHE TOSTADA

with Chipotle Oil

SERVES 4

6 oz (170 g) sea scallops

CEVICHE

¼ cup (60 mL) lime juice

¼ red onion, sliced

½ tsp (2.5 mL) salt

2 Tbsp (30 mL) chopped cilantro

CHIPOTLE OIL

½ cup (125 mL) grapeseed oil

1 Tbsp (15 mL) chipotle powder

½ tsp (2.5 mL) salt

1 tsp (5 mL) paprika

TOSTADAS

2 cups (500 mL) vegetable oil

Four 4-inch (10 cm) tortilla shells

Salt, to taste

TOPPINGS

1 avocado, diced

1 radish, thinly sliced

1 jalapeño, thinly sliced

Cilantro, for garnish

Ceviche is such a wonderfully refreshing dish. It's honestly a sunset on a plate. Citrus, mild fish, and spicy chipotle oil drizzled onto a warm chip is a vacation in a bite.

I like to serve my ceviche on fried tortillas, which are the prefect crunchy vessel for the tender scallops. You get a little bit of everything in each bite.

"If life gives you limes, make ceviche."

Method

CEVICHE Dice the scallops into small ¼-inch (0.5 cm) cubes and place in a non-reactive container (not metal). Combine the lime juice, onion, salt, and cilantro and pour over the scallops, making sure all the seafood is submerged in the juices. Cover and let rest in the fridge for 20 minutes.

CHIPOTLE OIL Slowly heat all the chipotle oil ingredients in a small sauce-pan. Once the oil is hot, turn off the heat and allow to steep for 20 minutes. Strain through a coffee filter or cheesecloth and reserve.

TOSTADAS Heat 2 cups (500 mL) vegetable oil in a heavy-bottomed pot until it reaches 350°F (180°C). Place one tortilla at a time in the oil and fry until crispy. Remove and place on a kitchen towel–lined baking tray and season with salt. Repeat with the remaining tortillas.

Assembly

Once the scallops are ready, they will be opaque. Remove them from the marinade. Top the tostadas with the ceviche, diced avocado, thinly sliced radish, thinly sliced jalapeño, and cilantro. Drizzle with chipotle oil and serve.

. . . recipe continued

FISH TIP

In a ceviche, the fish is "cooked" by using citrus to cure the fish completely. This can take hours, but if you want to speed up the process, you can blanch the diced seafood quickly in simmering water and marinate right into the citrus juices. This will kick-start the "curing process."

SMOKED SALMON FLATBREAD

with Crispy Roasted Chickpeas / Quick Pickled Red Onion /
Tikka Masala Cream Cheese / Tamarind Drizzle

Flatbreads are super fun to make and fast, so lucky for us this recipe uses flatbread for the base. Flatbread brushed with oil and cooked in the oven until crispy is the perfect vessel for salmon lox, an ingredient with some pretty good friends—one of them being cream cheese. Mixed with the symphony of flavours of an Indian tikka masala, this flatbread is a game changer. The quick pickles give the dish a little "sunshine" and the tamarind drizzle makes for really exciting bites every time.

It's great for sharing no matter how you cut it. Serve on a wooden board or long platter and dive in.

"It's like an old friend with a new haircut."

Method

Preheat oven to 375°F (190°C).

CRISPY ROASTED CHICKPEAS Toss the chickpeas in a bowl with the olive oil, cumin, and salt. Spread the mixture on a parchment-lined baking sheet. Bake for 25 to 35 minutes, or unit golden brown and crispy. Remove and set aside until ready to use.

Raise the oven temperature to 400°F (200°C) for the flatbread.

QUICK PICKLED RED ONION Combine all quick pickled red onion ingredients in a small container with a lid. Shake well and let stand for 10 minutes.

TIKKA MASALA CREAM CHEESE Heat 1 tsp (5 mL) vegetable oil in a small skillet over medium heat. Add the onion and garlic and cook until translucent. In a mixing bowl, combine the cooked onion and garlic with the cream cheese and all the remaining tikka masala cream cheese ingredients. With a whisk, whip the mixture until smooth and creamy. Reserve at room temperature.

TAMARIND DRIZZLE Heat all the tamarind drizzle ingredients in a small saucepan or skillet over medium heat until the sugar has dissolved, about 2 minutes. Allow to cool.

FLATBREAD Lightly brush the flatbread with 1 tsp (5 mL) vegetable oil. Place on a baking sheet and bake for 10 minutes. Flip after 5 minutes and bake until both sides are crisp and golden brown.

. . . recipe continued

SERVES 2 TO 4

5 slices (85 g) smoked salmon lox

CRISPY ROASTED CHICKPEAS

⅓ cup (80 mL) canned chickpeas, drained

1 tsp (5 mL) olive oil

¼ tsp (1 mL) cumin

Pinch of salt

QUICK PICKLED RED ONION

1 medium shallot, thinly sliced

⅓ cup (80 mL) red wine vinegar

2 Tbsp (30 mL) sugar

¼ tsp (1 mL) salt

1 tsp (5 mL) cumin

1 Tbsp (15 mL) water

TIKKA MASALA CREAM CHEESE

1 tsp (5 mL) vegetable oil

1 Tbsp (15 mL) diced onion

1 tsp (5 mL) diced garlic

¼ cup + 2 Tbsp (90 mL) cream cheese, room temperature

¼ tsp (1 mL) turmeric

Pinch of cayenne

¼ tsp (1 mL) cumin

Pinch of clove powder

1 tsp (5 mL) shredded unsweetened coconut

¼ tsp (1 mL) lemon juice

¼ tsp (1 mL) salt

. . . ingredients continued

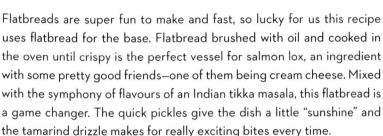

Assembly

TAMARIND DRIZZLE

2 Tbsp (30 mL) concentrated tamarind paste

3 Tbsp (45 mL) hot water

3 Tbsp (45 mL) brown sugar

½ tsp (2.5 mL) salt

1 tsp (5 mL) cumin

¼ tsp (1 mL) cayenne

FLATBREAD

One 8- × 4-inch (20 x 10 cm) flatbread

1 tsp (5 mL) vegetable oil

GARNISH

Cilantro (optional)

Chili oil (optional)

With a spatula, spread the cream cheese mixture over the cooled flatbread. Place salmon lox on top. I like to add the pickled red onion and finish with the tamarind drizzle and roasted chickpeas. The cilantro and chili oil are optional, but I find they add just the right touch of freshness and spice.

FISH TIP

This recipe works great with quality store-bought salmon lox. I like using coho lox. Coho salmon is a little more fatty than sockeye, and has a great taste. Even homemade smoked salmon flaked on top will work just fine. I use interleaf salmon because the parchment between the slices makes it easy to pull each piece apart without tearing it.

BRIOCHE SHRIMP TOAST

with Five-Spice Sweet and Sour Dip / Ginger Marmalade

½ lb (250 g) shrimp, peeled and deveined (see Fish Tip, page 201)

FIVE-SPICE SWEET AND SOUR DIP

1 Tbsp (15 mL) Worcestershire sauce

½ tsp (2.5 mL) soy sauce

¼ tsp (1 mL) five-spice powder

2 Tbsp (30 mL) plum sauce

GINGER MARMALADE

1 Tbsp (15 mL) minced ginger

¼ tsp (1 mL) sugar

2 Tbsp (30 mL) vegetable oil

Pinch of salt

1 Tbsp (15 mL) sliced green onion

SHRIMP PASTE

1 tsp (5 mL) sesame oil

1 Tbsp (15 mL) sliced green onion

2 tsp (10 mL) chopped ginger

1 egg white

½ tsp (2.5 mL) cornstarch

¼ tsp (1 mL) salt

4 slices brioche loaf

TOAST

1 cup (250 mL) vegetable oil

½ cup (125 mL) toasted black and white sesame seeds

As kids, we would go for dim sum on special occasions at the Regalia Restaurant with my dad during his lunch break. One of my favourite dishes was shrimp toast. It was a simple shrimp paste with luxurious sesame oil slathered on toast, dipped in sesame seeds and shallow-fried until crispy. It was crazy delicious. This is my version of shrimp toast. Like most things in life, the complicated is not always that complicated.

This is a dim sum–styled dish that is simple, delicious, and easy to grab. Stack them high with sauces on the side.

"Shrimp toast is like endless quarters in an arcade. Total joy."

Method

FIVE-SPICE SWEET AND SOUR DIP Stir all the five-spice sweet and sour dip ingredients together until well combined. Reserve for plating.

GINGER MARMALADE Stir all the ginger marmalade ingredients together until well combined and reserve.

SHRIMP PASTE Combine the shrimp and all the shrimp paste ingredients in a small food processor and pulse until a thick paste is achieved.

TOAST Heat 1 cup (250 mL) vegetable oil in a large skillet until it reaches 350°F (180°C).

Scatter the sesame seeds on a plate. Spread the shrimp paste from corner to corner on each slice of brioche toast. Press the shrimp side of each toast slice into the sesame seeds to coat.

Place two slices at a time into the hot oil and shallow-fry for 90 seconds per side until golden brown. Remove and continue with the remaining slices of toast.

Assembly

Cut each toast slice in half and stack. I serve the sauces on the side, just like they do for dim sum.

. . . recipe continued

FISH TIP

This recipe uses a food processor to chop the shrimp into a coarse paste. If you don't have a food processor, you can chop the shrimp by hand. I like to cut the shrimp in half lengthwise and rough chop until you get it to a paste consistency. Shrimp should always be ocean-friendly. I use peeled and deveined raw Pacific white shrimp, which might be a mouthful but it's the responsible choice, and it's just so good!

DUNGENESS CRAB FRITTERS

with Spicy Red Pepper Relish / Lemon Yogurt

If you're entertaining, pre-fry your crab fritters and warm them up in the oven just before serving. This gives you time to clean up, do your hair, pour a glass of bubbly, and, when you want fritters, just pop them into a warm oven for a few minutes. You'll look like a pro!

Line them up and knock 'em back. I plate the crab fritters on a round black slate. It makes the yogurt pop and the whole dish come alive, and it's perfect for sharing and passing around.

"Ah, yes! The crab fritter—it's like your birthday party in one bite of food."

Method

Pick through the crab carefully to remove any stray bits of shell. Add the crab to a medium-size bowl.

CRAB FRITTERS Add all the crab fritter ingredients, except the panko, to the bowl with the crab and stir to combine, being careful to keep the crab chunks intact. Add the panko and gently fold into the mix. Lightly pack the mix down and cover the bowl with plastic wrap. Place the mixture in the fridge for 20 minutes to firm up.

SPICY RED PEPPER RELISH Cook all the spicy red pepper relish ingredients in a pan over medium-low heat until all the liquid has evaporated, about 6 to 8 minutes. Reserve for plating.

LEMON YOGURT Combine all the lemon yogurt ingredients in a bowl and mix well. Chill until ready to serve.

BREADING Heat 4 cups (1 L) vegetable oil in a heavy-bottomed pot until it reaches 350°F (175°C).

In 3 medium-size bowls or inserts, set up a breading station for the fritters by placing each ingredient (flour, egg, and panko) in its own shallow bowl. Using a small ice cream scoop or 2 oz (60 mL) ladle, form the fritter mix into balls. Roll the fritters in the flour, then the egg, and finally the panko. Place the fritters gently into the hot oil; fry for 2 minutes or until golden brown and warm throughout. Place on a baking sheet lined with kitchen towels until ready to serve.

. . . recipe continued

SERVES 4 TO 6

½ lb (250 g) fresh Dungeness crab lump meat

CRAB FRITTERS

¼ cup (60 mL) corn kernels

¼ cup (60 mL) diced zucchini

1 tsp (5 mL) diced garlic

Pinch of cayenne

¼ tsp (1 mL) smoked paprika

¼ tsp (1 mL) curry powder

¼ tsp (1 mL) salt

¼ tsp (1 mL) pepper

3 Tbsp (45 mL) mayo

2 Tbsp (30 mL) chopped parsley

1 Tbsp (15 mL) panko breadcrumbs

SPICY RED PEPPER RELISH

¼ cup (60 mL) diced roasted red peppers

2 Tbsp (30 mL) diced shallots

¼ cup (60 mL) seeded and diced Roma tomatoes

½ tsp (2.5 mL) diced garlic

½ tsp (2.5 mL) diced ginger

¼ tsp (1 mL) cumin

¼ cup (60 mL) red wine vinegar

¼ cup (60 mL) brown sugar

¼ tsp (1 mL) salt

¼ tsp (1 mL) pepper

. . . ingredients continued

Assembly

LEMON YOGURT

¼ cup (60 mL) plain Greek yogurt

¼ cup (60 mL) sour cream

1 Tbsp (15 mL) lemon juice

¼ tsp (1 mL) salt

BREADING

4 cups (1 L) vegetable oil

1 cup (250 mL) flour

2 eggs, lightly beaten

1½ cups (375 mL) panko breadcrumbs

GARNISH

Chives, chopped

Dollop some of the lemon yogurt on a large plate for the crab fritters to rest in. Top each fritter with the red pepper relish and a little more yogurt. Finish with chopped chives and serve.

FISH TIP

Fresh Dungeness crab is one of the ocean's delicacies. If you can't find fresh, you can use canned—just make sure it's from a good source, and that you drain out excess water and check for little bits of shell. Use the same weight canned to fresh. When selecting fresh Dungeness crab at the fish market, ask for a little taste—if it's fresh, sweet, and firm, you're good to go.

SPICY "CRUNCH ROLL" ALBACORE TUNA POKE

*with Teriyaki Glaze / Crunchy Tempura Flakes /
Spicy Sriracha Mayo / Avocado–Mango Salsa*

SERVES 2 TO 4

6 oz (170 g) sashimi-grade
albacore tuna, diced into
½-inch (1 cm) cubes

1 cup (250 mL) uncooked
jasmine rice

TERIYAKI GLAZE

1 cup (250 mL) soy sauce

1 Tbsp (15 mL) sesame oil

½ cup (125 mL) brown sugar

1 Tbsp (15 mL) minced garlic

¼ tsp (1 mL) five-spice powder

1 Tbsp (15 mL) rice wine vinegar

1 Tbsp (15 mL) sake

Salt, to taste

3 Tbsp (45 mL) cornstarch

¼ cup (60 mL) water

CRUNCHY TEMPURA FLAKES

4 cups (1 L) vegetable oil

⅓ cup (80 mL) flour

½ cup (125 mL) cold club soda

1 egg white

¼ tsp (1 mL) salt

SPICY SRIRACHA MAYO

1 Tbsp (15 mL) sriracha

2 Tbsp (30 mL) mayonnaise

½ tsp (2.5 mL) sesame oil

1 tsp (5 mL) soy sauce

. . . ingredients continued

Poke is fish served raw and marinated, and this one is modelled after a crunchy sushi roll. It's spicy, sweet, and full of flavour and texture—a complete show.

This dish is fun to mould. I use a large metal ring mould, but if you don't have one you can use a round cookie cutter or small deli cup. You can serve this with any tortilla chip, light cracker, or even shrimp chips.

"Poke reminds me of Elvis performing in Aloha from Hawaii. *Super colourful, great tan, and just killing it. Aloha, Baby!"*

Method

Cook the jasmine rice according to the package instructions while preparing the recipe.

TERIYAKI GLAZE In a saucepan over medium heat, bring all the teriyaki glaze ingredients, except the cornstarch and water, to a light simmer. In a separate bowl, mix together the cornstarch and water to make a slurry. Add the slurry to the saucepan and gently whisk until the sauce becomes thick. Remove from heat and reserve.

CRUNCHY TEMPURA FLAKES Heat 4 cups (1 L) vegetable oil in a heavy-bottomed pot until it reaches 350°F (180°C).

Mix all the cruncy tempura flakes ingredients together, except for the salt, making sure you leave a few lumps in the batter (this will make it very crispy when fried). In 2 or 3 different batches, use a whisk to sprinkle the batter into the oil. When floating and crispy, remove the flakes from the oil with a steel mesh strainer and place on a tray lined with a kitchen towel. Season with salt.

SPICY SRIRACHA MAYO Combine all the spicy Sriracha mayo ingredients and mix well. Cover with plastic and refrigerate until ready to plate.

AVOCADO-MANGO SALSA Combine the diced mango and avocado in a bowl. Add the oil and lime juice and gently fold together. Cover with plastic and refrigerate until ready to plate.

. . . recipe continued

TUNA POKE MIX Add the diced tuna, white onion, green onion, and sesame seeds to a bowl and gently mix together. Fold in 1 Tbsp (15 mL) of the spicy Sriracha mayo and the salt.

Assembly

Take a 6-inch (15 cm) mould and fill the base with the cooked jasmine rice. Press it down with a spoon. Top with avocado–mango salsa and press again. Top that with the tuna poke mix and press once more. Carefully slide the mould up and off of the tuna stack. Top the tuna with crunchy tempura flakes, and garnish with pea shoots and sprouts. Drizzle with the teriyaki glaze and remaining spicy Sriracha mayo and serve.

FISH TIP

I usually find my albacore tuna in the freezer section, vacuum packed, which means it's ready to eat raw. If raw fish is not your thing, you can always dice and cook the tuna. Once cooked, you can then marinate it in the spicy mayo. This will also work with Ocean Wise sashimi-grade ahi tuna and even salmon. If you have any leftover sushi-grade tuna, wrap it in dry kitchen towels then plastic wrap. This will keep the tuna dry and healthy in the fridge for a few days.

AVOCADO–MANGO SALSA

⅓ cup (80 mL) diced mango
(½-inch/1 cm cubes)

⅓ cup (80 mL) diced avocado
(½-inch/1 cm cubes)

½ tsp (2.5 mL) grapeseed oil

½ tsp (2.5 mL) lime juice

TUNA POKE MIX

1 Tbsp (15 mL) diced white onion

1 Tbsp (15 mL) sliced green onion

½ tsp (2.5 mL) black sesame seeds

½ tsp (2.5 mL) white sesame seeds

¼ tsp (1 mL) salt

GARNISH

Pea shoots

Sprouts

BLACKENED AHI TUNA TATAKI

with Red Slaw / Creole Mustard Vinaigrette

Tuna tataki is in the building! The rich and deep flavours of blackening spice work so well with the meaty texture of the tuna. Let this tuna take a dive into the Creole mustard vinaigrette and you will understand the true meaning of delicious.

I let the tuna shine on white china, and my preferred shape for plating is a long rectangular or oval dish. This will give you the maximum tuna-to-dressing ratio, and it's nice to eat with your eyes first.

"Phenomenal cosmic flavour . . . itty bitty living space."

Method

RED SLAW Place the shredded cabbage in a bowl. Add the mayonnaise, hot sauce, vinegar, sugar, and salt.

Add the tomatoes and gently toss to bring together. Set aside.

CREOLE MUSTARD VINAIGRETTE Combine all the Creole mustard vinaigrette ingredients, except the oil, in a small bowl. While continuously whisking, drizzle in the oil until smooth. Reserve.

BLACKENING SPICE Combine all the blackening spice ingredients in a bowl and mix until well combined. Set aside.

AHI TUNA TATAKI Season the tuna with ¼ tsp (1 mL) salt. Place the blackening spice on a plate and press both sides of the tuna into the spice. Heat 1 Tbsp (15 mL) vegetable oil in a skillet over high heat. Place the tuna in the pan for 30 seconds on each side. The outside will cook while the inside should remain rare.

Assembly

Arrange the red slaw down one side of the plate in a vertical line. Slice the tuna against the grain and fan it out beside the slaw. Spoon the Creole mustard vinaigrette around the tuna and garnish with a few sprouts.

. . . *recipe continued*

SERVES 2 TO 4

6 oz (170 g) sashimi-grade ahi tuna

¼ tsp (1 mL) salt

1 Tbsp (15 mL) vegetable oil

RED SLAW

2 cups (500 mL) shredded red cabbage

2 Tbsp (30 mL) mayonnaise

½ tsp (2.5 mL) hot sauce

¼ tsp (1 mL) white wine vinegar

½ tsp (2.5 mL) sugar

Salt, to taste

¼ cup (60 mL) cherry tomatoes, quartered

CREOLE MUSTARD VINAIGRETTE

1 Tbsp (15 mL) grainy Dijon mustard

Pinch of seafood seasoning

1 tsp (5 mL) smoked paprika

2 Tbsp (30 mL) white wine vinegar

1 Tbsp (15 mL) water

1½ Tbsp (22 mL) honey

⅛ tsp (0.5 mL) salt (a dash)

5 Tbsp (75 mL) grapeseed oil

. . . ingredients continued

BLACKENING SPICE

¼ tsp (1 mL) kosher salt

1 Tbsp (15 mL) smoked paprika

½ tsp (2.5 mL) garlic powder

½ tsp (2.5 mL) onion powder

¼ tsp (1 mL) mustard powder

1 tsp (5 mL) sesame seeds

1 Tbsp (15 mL) chili powder

GARNISH

Pea shoots or sprouts

FISH TIP

When I'm looking for ahi tuna, I always ask if it is sustainable/ocean-friendly, as well as whether it's sashimi-grade. If not, I like to use albacore tuna, which I usually find in the frozen section of the fish market. It's a perfect sustainable alternative. When selecting tuna, try to get a "centre cut," as this will help the fish cook evenly. Remember to slice against the grain.

BAKED MUSSELS ON THE HALF SHELL

with Chipotle Butter / Herbed Breadcrumbs

1 lb (450 g) fresh mussels

Half a lemon, seared in a skillet or on a grill until lightly charred, for serving

CHIPOTLE BUTTER

½ cup (125 mL) unsalted butter, room temperature

1 egg yolk

1 tsp (5 mL) diced chipotle pepper

1 tsp (5 mL) lemon zest

½ tsp (2.5 mL) lemon juice

¼ tsp (1 mL) smoked paprika

¼ tsp (1 mL) salt

HERBED BREADCRUMBS

2 Tbsp (30 mL) unsalted butter, room temperature

¼ cup (60 mL) panko breadcrumbs

1 Tbsp (15 mL) lemon zest

1 Tbsp (15 mL) chopped parsley

¼ tsp (1 mL) chili flakes

1 tsp (5 mL) minced garlic

I can't get enough of these baked mussels. They can be made ahead of time and popped in the oven when you're ready to eat, and they're great for entertaining, or even on a Wednesday afternoon. They are that good! The chipotle butter has the perfect kick of spice to go with the sweetness of the mussels, and the crunchy breadcrumbs will have you coming back for more.

I bake these little gems on crumpled aluminum foil on a baking sheet to keep the mussels from tipping. I like to serve them on clean craft river rocks that I cover in boiling water for a few minutes. The rocks get hot and help keep the mussels warm.

"On your mark, get set, mussel!"

Method

Clean the mussels: Remove beards and wash the shells. In a sauce pot with a tight fitting lid, add ¼ cup (60 mL) water and the mussels, cover, and steam on medium to high heat for about 2 to 3 minutes. Strain and discard any that do not open. Allow to slightly cool while preparing the chipotle butter and herbed breadcrumbs.

CHIPOTLE BUTTER Combine all the chipotle butter ingredients in a bowl and mix until smooth. Keep at room temperature.

HERBED BREADCRUMBS Melt 2 Tbsp (30 mL) butter in a frying pan. Add the remaining herbed breadcrumb ingredients and toast for 1 to 2 minutes until lightly golden brown. Keep at room temperature.

MUSSELS Preheat oven to a low broil.

Place a crumpled piece of aluminum foil onto a baking tray. Remove the "lid" of each mussel and, using a butter knife, loosen the mussel from the base shell, but leave it resting inside. Using a spoon, fill each mussel with chipotle butter, right to the rim. Coat the top of each mussel with the herbed breadcrumbs and place under the broiler for 2 to 3 minutes. I recommend checking every 30 seconds so you don't burn them. Remove when golden brown.

. . . recipe continued

Assembly

I serve the mussels on warm river rocks. I cover the rocks in boiling water, gently pour the rocks onto a plate or tray, then add the mussels around the grilled lemon.

FISH TIP

Believe it or not, some mussels have beards, and you want to give them a "shave." You can simply pull away the beard or use a toothpick. Make sure the outside shells are scrubbed clean, and discard any mussels that are open.

FRESH SHUCKED OYSTERS

with Rosé Mignonette / Wasabi–Maple Vinaigrette / Seafood Sauce

Fresh shucked oysters are such a celebration. They are the jewels of the ocean! Oysters will dance on their own, but in this recipe I had some fun with the condiments.

I plate the oysters on broken ice. If the oysters come in a box, use the box as a vessel. It looks so fun and adds to the celebration.

"You know it's good if it's ordered by the dozen."

Method

ROSÉ MIGNONETTE Combine all the rosé mignonette ingredients in a bowl and mix well. Place the sauce in a ramekin for guests to drizzle over the tops of the oysters as they wish.

WASABI–MAPLE VINAIGRETTE Combine all the wasabi–maple vinaigrette ingredients in a bowl and mix to combine. Serve in a ramekin.

SEAFOOD SAUCE Combine all the seafood sauce ingredients in a bowl and mix to combine. Serve in a ramekin.

Assembly

Shuck the oysters (see Fish Tip following recipe) and place them on a bed of ice. Surround them with the sauces, fresh lemon, and seafood forks. Enjoy!

. . . recipe continued

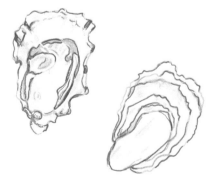

SERVES 6

12 fresh oysters

Fresh lemon wedge, for serving

ROSÉ MIGNONETTE

1 medium shallot, diced

1 tsp (5 mL) pepper

¼ cup (60 mL) rosé

2 Tbsp (30 mL) red wine vinegar

3 Tbsp (45 mL) chives

¼ tsp (1 mL) salt

¼ tsp (1 mL) sugar

WASABI–MAPLE VINAIGRETTE

1 tsp (5 mL) wasabi paste

3 Tbsp (45 mL) lemon juice

1 Tbsp (15 mL) grapeseed oil

½ tsp (2.5 mL) maple syrup

1 Tbsp (15 mL) diced shallots

SEAFOOD SAUCE

½ cup (125 mL) ketchup

1 Tbsp (15 mL) lemon juice

½ tsp (2.5 mL) seafood seasoning

½ tsp (2.5 mL) smoked paprika

2 Tbsp (30 mL) prepared horseradish

2 Tbsp (30 mL) chopped chives

FISH TIP

The best way to shuck an oyster is to do it with some confidence. Hold the oyster with a towel and use your strong hand to gently rock and work the tip of the oyster knife into the hinge of the oyster, where the top and bottom shells meet. It's like turning a key—you can't force it! Once you have worked the top off, clean the knife and run the knife along the flat edge of the oyster to release the muscle that is attached to the shell. Clean the knife again and free the oyster from the shell. Enjoy!

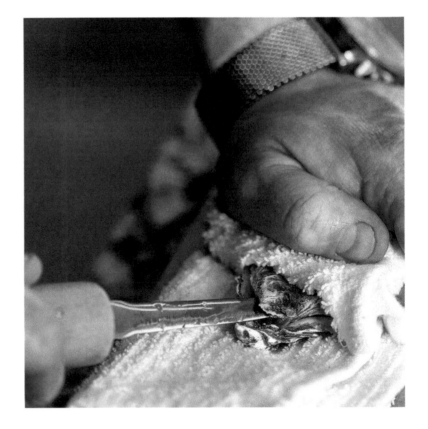

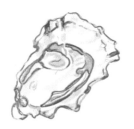

CORNMEAL FRIED POPCORN OYSTERS

with Horse-Ranchish Dipping Sauce

SERVES 4

24 fresh medium-size oysters

Hot sauce, for serving

Lemons, for serving

BUTTERMILK MARINADE

⅔ cup (160 mL) buttermilk

1 Tbsp (15 mL) hot sauce

HORSE-RANCHISH DIPPING SAUCE

1⅓ cups (330 mL) sour cream

1 Tbsp (15 mL) buttermilk

¼ cup (60 mL) mayonnaise

1 tsp (5 mL) dried dill

½ tsp (2.5 mL) minced garlic

¼ tsp (1 mL) onion powder

1 tsp (5 mL) horseradish

½ tsp (2.5 mL) white wine vinegar

¼ tsp (1 mL) sugar

¼ tsp (1 mL) salt

½ tsp (2.5 mL) pepper

DRY DREDGE

4 cups (1 L) vegetable oil

½ cup (125 mL) flour

¼ cup (60 mL) cornmeal

½ tsp (2.5 mL) salt
+ more as needed

¼ tsp (1 mL) pepper

½ tsp (2.5 mL) paprika

½ tsp (2.5 mL) onion powder

½ tsp (2.5 mL) garlic powder

This is a perfect oyster dish for a late afternoon as the sun sets and you're feeling like a delicious snack. They are perfect because they're crispy, bite-size, and delicious. The only problem is they seem to disappear in the blink of an eye.

I love how seafood can be dressed to impress or dressed down for the beach. I like to serve these beach-style all the way: simple, casual, and delicious. Find a box, a basket, or a paper cone, grab some lemons, and this is one humble oyster snack.

"These popcorn oysters are so good, my grandmother immediately drove to my house when I told her I was making them . . . funny thing, my grandmother lost her license and doesn't own a vehicle . . . oops!"

Method

Shuck all the oysters (see Fish Tip, page 36). Discard the shells.

BUTTERMILK MARINADE Combine the buttermilk and hot sauce in a bowl. Add the shucked oysters and allow them to soak for 10 minutes in the refrigerator.

HORSE-RANCHISH DIPPING SAUCE Mix all the horse-ranchish dipping sauce ingredients together in a bowl until well combined. Set aside.

DRY DREDGE Heat 4 cups (1 L) vegetable oil in a heavy-bottomed pot or Dutch oven until it reaches 375°F (190°C).

Combine the flour, cornmeal, and spices together in a container with a lid (Tupperware works wonders). Remove the oysters from the buttermilk mixture and place in the dry dredge mix. Shake until well coated.

Gently lower the oysters into the frying oil. Cook for about 1 minute until golden brown. Remove to a tray lined with a kitchen towel and season with salt.

Assembly

Serve oysters warm with the horse-ranchish dipping sauce and your favourite hot sauce—and don't forget the lemon.

. . . recipe continued

FISH TIP

Believe it or not, you can pre-shuck oysters up to 2 hours before you eat them. I like to line a cookie sheet with wet kitchen towels and shuck the oysters using that. When they're done, I place a damp kitchen towel over them and pop them in the fridge. When you're ready to eat, place the oysters on some crushed ice and get into it!

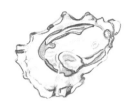

OVEN-BROILED SWEET MISO OYSTERS

with Sautéed Spinach / Chili Breadcrumbs

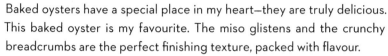

Baked oysters have a special place in my heart—they are truly delicious. This baked oyster is my favourite. The miso glistens and the crunchy breadcrumbs are the perfect finishing texture, packed with flavour.

I plate this on a bed of coarse sea salt with some wild herbs or lettuce. Crumpled parchment paper will also work in a pinch.

"Don't get me wrong, raw oysters are amazing, but if I placed a raw apple and an apple pie beside each other, which one would you eat? Just saying . . ."

Method

Preheat oven to 400°F (200°C).

SAUTÉED SPINACH Melt the butter in a frying pan over medium heat. Add the spinach, ginger, shallots, and salt, and drizzle with sesame oil. Cover with a lid for 30 seconds to wilt. Remove the cover and, using tongs, move the spinach around until wilted and bright green. Drain the spinach on a tray lined with kitchen towels.

MISO SAUCE In a bowl, mix together all the miso sauce ingredients except for the oil. Add the oil slowly while whisking, until the sauce is thick and smooth. Reserve.

CHILI BREADCRUMBS Melt the butter in a pan over medium heat. Add the garlic, panko, lemon zest, and spices and toast for 1 to 2 minutes until golden. Keep at room temperature.

OYSTERS Fill a small baking tray with about 4 cups (1 L) coarse salt. Shuck the oysters (see Fish Tip, page 36). Discard the tops and run your knife under each oyster to loosen it from its base. Place the open oysters (in the bottom shells) on the salt.

Divide the sautéed spinach evenly among the 4 oysters. Top with the miso sauce and place in the oven to bake for 12 minutes. Once the oysters are cooked, sprinkle with the chili breadcrumbs and serve immediately.

Assembly

Serve the oysters on a rustic plate covered with sea salt and wild herbs.

SERVES 2 TO 4

4 fresh medium-size oysters

4 cups (1 L) salt (approx.)

SAUTÉED SPINACH

1 Tbsp (15 mL) unsalted butter

2 cups (500 mL) spinach

2 tsp (10 mL) diced ginger

1 tsp (5 mL) diced shallots

¼ tsp (1 mL) salt

1 tsp (5 mL) sesame oil

MISO SAUCE

1 Tbsp (15 mL) white miso

1 tsp (5 mL) soy sauce

1 Tbsp (15 mL) white sugar

½ tsp (2.5 mL) lemon juice

1 egg yolk

¼ cup (60 mL) grapeseed oil

CHILI BREADCRUMBS

1 Tbsp (15 mL) unsalted butter

2 tsp (10 mL) minced garlic

¼ cup (60 mL) panko breadcrumbs

1 Tbsp (15 mL) lemon zest

¼ tsp (1 mL) chili flakes

½ tsp (2.5 mL) dried thyme

GARNISH

Coarse salt

Baby greens and fresh herbs of your choice

. . . recipe continued

FISH TIP

When oysters are baked, they shrink up, so it's better not to use the petit oysters. Plus, with a slightly larger oyster, there is more room for goodies! I like to bake these on a bed of rock salt. It holds the oysters upright, keeping all the garnish inside.

CHAPTER NO. 2

SOUPS & GREENS

Soups and salads are fantastic. Soups can have so much flavour, it's almost silly.
In this section, I made some really fun and approachable recipes for soups and salads, some
twists on old classics, and some new heavy hitters!

"BIG CATCH" SEAFOOD CHOWDER 48

with Lobster Tails / Clams / Cod / Bacon

CREOLE SHELLFISH BISQUE 53

with Lump Crab Cake / Vegetable Confetti

THAI-STYLE SEAFOOD "BOUILLABAISSE" 56

with Walleye / Jumbo Shrimp / Mussels / Spicy Coconut Broth

HALIBUT & PRAWN RED CURRY 61

with Coconut Milk / Potatoes / Snap Peas

"BROKE DOWN" SCALLOP WONTON SOUP 64

with Szechuan Chili Broth

PAN-SEARED HADDOCK IN INDIAN SPICED BROTH 69

with Spiced Tomato Chutney / Roasted Onions / Braised Kale

ANGLERS LUNCH 72

*with Ramen Eggs / Quinoa Salad / Crunchy Vegetables /
Shiitake Mushroom Vinaigrette / Soft-Baked Salmon*

WARM LOBSTER POTATO SALAD 77

*with Braised Bacon / Sun-Dried Tomato and Tarragon Vinaigrette /
Asparagus / Fingerling Potatoes*

TEX MEX-RUBBED HALIBUT TACO SALAD 80

*with Rice and Beans / Santa Fe Salsa / Cocoa Taco Sauce /
Smashed Avocado*

"SMOKED" TROUT & SESAME SPINACH SALAD 85

with Sweet Sesame Dressing / Wasabi Popcorn

"BIG CATCH" SEAFOOD CHOWDER

with Lobster Tails / Clams / Cod / Bacon

SERVES 4

3½ oz (105 g) precooked lobster tails, cut into 1-inch (2.5 cm) pieces

½ lb (250 g) clams

5 oz (155 g) cod, cut into 1-inch (2.5 cm) pieces

CHOWDER

1 Tbsp (15 mL) olive oil

6 strips of thick-cut smoked bacon, large dice

1 cup (250 mL) diced onion

1 cup (250 mL) diced celery

1 tsp (5 mL) salt, divided

2 Tbsp (30 mL) unsalted butter

⅓ cup + 2 Tbsp (110 mL) all-purpose flour

3 cups (750 mL) fish stock

2½ cups (625 mL) water

2 cups (500 mL) full cream (35%)

2 cups (500 mL) cubed potatoes

½ cup (125 mL) corn

½ tsp (2.5 mL) Worcestershire sauce

½ tsp (2.5 mL) pepper

GARNISH

Chopped chives

Chili oil

There is something to be said about a big bowl of homemade chowder. It soothes the soul, and my favourite types of soups have lots of goodies in them, so naturally this one is packed with great seafood. Lobster and clams give the chowder some sweetness. Round out all that great fish with some thick-cut smoky bacon and potatoes and, on a cool day, this will make you feel amazing.

With a family-size portion of this on the table, a big ladle, and some crusty bread, there would be fights in my house to see who gets the last drop.

"If folding laundry ended with a bowl of this chowder, I would never leave the laundry room."

Method

Heat a heavy-bottomed pot or Dutch oven over medium-high heat. Add 1 Tbsp (15 mL) olive oil and the diced bacon. Allow the bacon to render and become golden brown and crisp. Add the onion, celery, and ½ tsp (2.5 mL) salt, then add the butter and let it melt; add the flour and stir into the butter to make a roux. Cook for 1 minute until the butter and flour are well combined and turning golden.

Whisk the fish stock into the roux until combined. Add the water and cream. Add the potatoes and simmer lightly until they are almost fully cooked. Add all the seafood and the corn and cook for 2 to 3 minutes until the fish is cooked. Finish with the Worcestershire sauce, pepper, and the remaining salt.

Assembly

Scoop hearty ladles of chowder into your favourite deep bowls, and finish with chopped chives and a drizzle of chili oil.

. . . recipe continued

FISH TIP

Clams can come in many shapes and varieties, such as fresh, frozen, and canned. All of the above are great for a chowder. When selecting frozen or canned clams, try and look for ocean-friendly choices and clams that are harvested close to where you live. If you can't find the fish I used in this recipe, you can use almost any kind of fish you love: cod, salmon, haddock, mussels. I often use smoked fish, like smoked sablefish—delicious!

CREOLE SHELLFISH BISQUE

with Lump Crab Cake / Vegetable Confetti

I always save my lobster and prawn shells (including heads) whenever I can. They freeze unbelievably well, holding lots of flavour, and it doesn't take long before you have enough to make a great bisque. This one is very simple but isn't lacking the wow factor! I love the flavour that the Creole spices add to the rich soup, with the texture of a flaky lump crab cake. It will win the award for bite of the night.

I serve this bisque in a low-sided bowl. If you want to get really fancy, you can plate the crab cake and the vegetable confetti in the bowl and serve the bisque tableside from a teapot or gravy boat. Phones will be out taking pics in no time, so make sure not to spill!

"I have never wanted to be a spoon so bad in my life."

Method

Preheat oven to 375°F (190°C).

CREOLE SHELLFISH BISQUE Heat 2 Tbsp (30 mL) vegetable oil in a heavy-bottomed pot over medium heat. Add the onion, celery, garlic, and peppers and sauté until they start to sweat. Add your prawn shells, lobster heads, fennel seed, seafood seasoning, smoked paprika, chili powder, and sauté. Season the vegetables with salt. Add the tomato paste and stir. Add the fish stock and cream. Cook on low for 20 to 30 minutes while you prepare the crab cakes.

LUMP CRAB CAKE Beat the egg white to stiff peaks. Fold the crab meat and seafood seasoning together and form into 2 cakes. Place them on a parchment-lined baking sheet and bake for 5 minutes. Keep warm until ready to serve.

VEGETABLE CONFETTI Melt the butter in a skillet over medium heat. Add the diced vegetables and a pinch of salt and reduce heat to low. Warm the vegetables, leaving them with crunch and colour, and set aside.

BISQUE Strain the soup into a clean pot with a fine sieve. Keep warm over low heat until ready to serve.

... recipe continued

SERVES 2

6 oz (170 g) Dungeness lump crab meat

20 prawn shells

2 lobster heads

CREOLE SHELLFISH BISQUE

2 Tbsp (30 mL) vegetable oil

½ cup (125 mL) finely diced onion

¼ cup (60 mL) finely diced celery

1 Tbsp (15 mL) diced garlic

1 cup (250 mL) diced green pepper

1 cup (250 mL) diced red pepper

1 Tbsp (15 mL) fennel seed

1¾ tsp (9 mL) seafood seasoning

½ tsp (2.5 mL) smoked paprika

½ tsp (2.5 mL) chili powder

1 tsp (5 mL) salt

3 Tbsp (45 mL) tomato paste

1½ cups (375 mL) fish stock

2 cups (500 mL) heavy cream

LUMP CRAB CAKE

1 egg white

¼ tsp (1 mL) seafood seasoning

VEGETABLE CONFETTI

1 tsp (5 mL) unsalted butter

¼ cup (60 mL) diced green pepper

¼ cup (60 mL) diced red pepper

¼ cup (60 mL) finely diced onion

¼ cup (60 mL) finely diced celery

Pinch of salt

GARNISH

Sprouts

Assembly

Place the crab cake in the centre of a bowl. Place the vegetable confetti around the crab cake and garnish with sprouts. Pour the bisque into the bowl and enjoy.

FISH TIP

This recipe can be used with a variation of shells. You can mix and match as you please, just use the same weight as in the recipe. I freeze my shells in freezer-safe containers and fill them with cold tap water—that way they can stay in the freezer for a long time. Make sure you always label and date.

THAI-STYLE SEAFOOD "BOUILLABAISSE"

with Walleye / Jumbo Shrimp / Mussels / Spicy Coconut Broth

SERVES 4

6 oz (170 g) walleye (or white fish), cut into 1-inch (2.5 cm) pieces

1 lb (450 g) mussels, cleaned

6 jumbo shrimp, peeled and deveined (see Fish Tip, page 201)

SPICE PASTE

2 large red chilies

Pinch of saffron

2 Tbsp (30 mL) chopped ginger

1 Tbsp (15 mL) diced garlic

1 small shallot, sliced

1 tsp (5 mL) sugar

BOUILLABAISSE

4 fingerling potatoes, sliced into ½-inch (1 cm) coins

2 Tbsp (30 mL) vegetable oil

1 cup (250 mL) sliced shiitake mushrooms

1 cup (250 mL) chopped fennel

2 kaffir lime leaves

3 cups (750 mL) fish stock

1½ cups (375 mL) coconut milk

¼ tsp (1 mL) fish sauce

¼ tsp (1 mL) salt

¼ cup (60 mL) cilantro, chopped

¼ cup (60 mL) Thai basil, thinly sliced

1 Tbsp (15 mL) lime juice

GARNISH

Lime wedges

This soup is everything I love about cooking. It has colour, texture, and every flavour in the soup works so well together that magic happens when you take a bite. Every sensation your mouth can register seems to happen all at once. It's simple yet so exciting.

If you have a gnarly pot or serving dish from a grandmother or a garage sale, get it ready. This soup has character, and so should the serving vessel.

"If this soup was a boxing glove, I would willingly get punched in the face by it."

Method

SPICE PASTE Combine all the spice paste ingredients in a small food chopper or processor. Pulse until a coarse paste is achieved and reserve.

BOUILLABAISSE Cook the potatoes in a pot of boiling water until fork tender. Drain the water and let the potatoes cool slightly.

Heat 2 Tbsp (30 mL) vegetable oil in a hot skillet. Add the shiitake mushrooms and cook for 1 minute. Add the fennel and sauté for 2 minutes, then add the spice paste and sauté for another 2 minutes, stirring occasionally. Add the lime leaves, fish stock, coconut milk, and fish sauce and simmer for 10 minutes. Add all the seafood and cooked potatoes. Cover with a lid and simmer for 2 minutes, or until the fish is cooked and mussels are open. Discard any mussels that do not open. Finish with the salt, cilantro, basil, and lime juice.

Assembly

I plate the fish first in a clean serving vessel. Once I have it organized in a nice fashion, I spoon the soup overtop and garnish with lime wedges and any leftover herbs.

. . . recipe continued

FISH TIP

When I am buying shrimp for this recipe, I always make sure they are pdv, which means peeled and deveined. If using frozen shrimp, set them on a kitchen towel–lined plate and put them straight into the fridge. This will let them "slack-thaw," allowing them to gradually defrost overnight. Then you're good to go the next morning.

HALIBUT & PRAWN RED CURRY

with Coconut Milk / Potatoes / Snap Peas

Halibut and prawns have great texture and a mild taste that loves to pair with bold-flavour friends. Serve them in a bath of beautiful curry full of spices and the balance of heat, sweet, and sour makes the halibut and prawns sing. Finished with a kiss of luxurious coconut milk, if you ever doubted fish and curry this is your time to believe.

Serving it in a dark-coloured bowl gives this curry a magnificent look. I love the contrast of the red sauce and white coconut milk. It looks so inviting and just draws you in. Serve it with your favourite naan bread, and drop the mic.

"This curry is as comforting as having Morgan Freeman as your GPS voice."

Method

Preheat oven to 400°F (200°C).

RED CURRY Melt the butter in a skillet over medium heat. Add the onion and cook for 60 seconds until slightly translucent. Add the ginger and garlic and sauté for 30 seconds. Add all the dry spices and toast for 10 seconds, then add the Roma tomatoes and cook for another minute. Add the crushed tomatoes, fish stock, chickpeas, coconut milk, potatoes, sambal oelek, and salt. Lightly simmer until the potatoes are tender, approximately 8 to 10 minutes, stirring occasionally. Reserve.

HALIBUT Heat 2 Tbsp (30 mL) olive oil in a pan over high heat. Season the fish with ¼ tsp (1 mL) salt. Sear the halibut for 1 minute, then place in the oven for 3 to 5 minutes to finish cooking.

SNAP PEAS Simmer 1 cup (250 mL) water and salt in a small saucepan over low heat. Add the snap peas and blanch for 1 minute. Remove from water, cool, and reserve for plating.

HALIBUT CONTINUED When the halibut is 1 minute from coming out of the oven, add the shrimp to the red curry and cook at a light simmer for 1 minute.

. . . recipe continued

SERVES 4

12 oz (340 g) halibut fillet

4 oz (125 g) shrimp, peeled and deveined (see Fish Tip, page 201)

2 Tbsp (30 mL) olive oil

¼ tsp (1 mL) salt

RED CURRY

2 Tbsp (30 mL) unsalted butter

1 cup (250 mL) diced onion

2 Tbsp (30 mL) diced ginger

1 Tbsp (15 mL) diced garlic

½ tsp (2.5 mL) cumin

½ tsp (2.5 mL) garam masala

Pinch of cloves

¼ tsp (1 mL) cinnamon

¼ tsp (1 mL) turmeric

2 cups (500 mL) coarsely chopped Roma tomatoes

1 cup (250 mL) crushed tomatoes

1 cup (250 mL) fish stock

⅓ cup (80 mL) chickpeas

1 Tbsp (15 mL) coconut milk

1 cup (250 mL) raw, peeled, thick-cut potatoes

1 tsp (5 mL) sambal oelek

1 tsp (5 mL) salt

SNAP PEAS

¼ tsp (1 mL) salt

1 cup (250 mL) snap peas, cleaned and halved

GARNISH

Cilantro leaves

Coconut milk

Assembly

Ladle the red curry into small bowls. Add the halibut in the middle of the bowl, scatter the snap peas around with cilantro, and finish with a drizzle of coconut milk.

FISH TIP

When selecting halibut fillets, I try and find "thick-cut" centre pieces because halibut doesn't have a lot of natural fat. A thicker piece of halibut will cook more evenly and is a little more forgiving.

Remember to always serve hot fish right away.

It's the mid 90s and as my dad works around the boat I'm doing whatever I can to get him to laugh, turns out I'm just being annoying.

"BROKE DOWN" SCALLOP WONTON SOUP

with Szechuan Chili Broth

½ lb (250 g) bay scallops

SZECHUAN CHILI BROTH

1 tsp (5 mL) vegetable oil

1 Tbsp (15 mL) minced ginger

1 Tbsp (15 mL) minced garlic

¼ tsp (1 mL) allspice

½ tsp (2.5 mL) five-spice powder

1 Tbsp (15 mL) paprika

½ tsp (2.5 mL) chili flakes
+ more as needed

1 Tbsp + 1 tsp (20 mL) soy sauce

1 tsp (5 mL) rice wine vinegar

¼ tsp (1 mL) sesame oil

1 Tbsp (15 mL) chili oil

1 cup (250 mL) fish stock

2 cups (500 mL) dark chicken stock

2½ tsp (12.5 mL) sugar

SCALLOP WONTONS

1 tsp (5 mL) chopped ginger

1 tsp (5 mL) chopped garlic

1 tsp (5 mL) sliced green onion

1 tsp (5 mL) soy sauce

1 Tbsp (15 mL) cornstarch

1 tsp (5 mL) sesame seeds

½ tsp (2.5 mL) sesame oil

¼ tsp (1 mL) salt

12 to 20 square wonton wrappers

GARNISH

Roasted peanuts (store-bought), crushed

Green onion, thinly sliced

This little bowl of heaven is a riff on a classic wonton soup, hence the name "Broke Down." There are scallop-stuffed wontons, lots of peanuts, and green onions, and the broth is so flavourful you could drink it on its own. This soup is packed with umami and crunch, and it's almost too tasty. It's super easy to build big bold flavour quickly, and this soup is the mascot of that very thought.

I serve this in a small bowl. I find it looks crazy cool when the bowl is stuffed with goodness, and it also keeps the soup hot to the last spoonful.

"I'll take soup for $1,000, Alex!"

Method

SZECHUAN CHILI BROTH Heat 1 tsp (5 mL) vegetable oil in a saucepan over medium-high heat. Add the ginger and garlic and sauté for 1 minute, then reduce heat to medium and add the allspice, five-spice powder, paprika, and chili flakes and stir them in. Add the soy sauce, rice wine vinegar, sesame oil, chili oil, fish and chicken stocks, and sugar. Stir to combine and lightly simmer for 5 to 10 minutes. Keep warm.

SCALLOP WONTONS Toss the scallops and all the scallop wonton ingredients into a small food processor/mini chopper and blitz into a chunky paste. Lay the wonton wrappers on your counter and place a spoonful of the scallop mixture in the centre of each wonton square. Dip you finger in water and moisten the edges of a wrapper, then fold each wonton wrapper over its scallop mixture from corner to corner, to make a triangle. Press gently on the edges to seal. Dip your finger in the water again and moisten the corners at the widest part of each triangle, then curl them together so that they meet. Pinch. Repeat with the remaining wontons.

Add the wontons to the broth and cook for 2 minutes on a light simmer, covered.

Assembly

Add the scallop wontons and Szechuan chili broth to your favourite bowls, garnish with chopped roasted peanuts and sliced green onions. If you want an extra kick, add a touch more chili flakes.

. . . recipe continued

When we were fishing, I was always the guy who watched the rods to see if fish were biting. This was also a perfect time to catch a little nap once and a while.

FISH TIP

When using scallops of any kind, make sure you remove the side mussel. This is very chewy and almost inedible. I look through all my scallops before cooking and peel off any that I see.

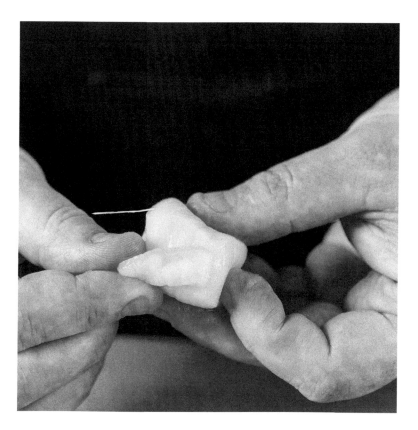

PAN-SEARED HADDOCK IN INDIAN SPICED BROTH

with Spiced Tomato Chutney / Roasted Shallots / Braised Kale

Curry as a broth? Yup! This recipe is about to rock your world. The natural sweetness of the haddock is perfect for this punchy, fragrant broth with a rich beef base and warm spices. It sounds crazy, but the spiced beef broth works so well with fish. Loaded with kale, charred onions, soft beans, and a spicy, tangy, chewy tomato chutney, this soup is the genie in the lamp.

Serving this in a rustic bowl gives the curry a magnificent look. I love the contrast of the red chutney, golden fish, and dark colours of the onions and kale. It's a feast for the senses.

"You ain't never had a friend like me."

Method

Preheat oven to 400°F (200°C)

INDIAN SPICED BROTH Heat 1 Tbsp (15 mL) olive oil in a heavy-bottomed pot over medium to high heat, then add the fennel seeds, ginger, shallot, and garlic. Sauté for 90 seconds, reduce heat to medium, and add all the dry spices, salt, and sugar; toast for 20 seconds while stirring. Add the beef broth and gently simmer for 10 to 15 minutes. Add the butter and chili oil, and keep the broth hot for plating.

SPICED TOMATO CHUTNEY Combine all the spiced tomato chutney ingredients in a skillet over medium heat, stir, and cook until all the moisture has evaporated. Set aside.

ROASTED SHALLOTS Cut your shallots in half, leaving the bases intact; leave the skin on. Add 1 tsp (5 mL) vegetable oil and ¼ tsp (1 mL) salt to a skillet over high heat and sear the shallots, cut side down, for 1 minute. Cook in the oven for 8 minutes, until soft.

Slide the skins off and set aside until ready to plate.

BRAISED KALE Add the butter, kale, and ginger to a frying pan and sauté for 1 minute. Add the beans and cook until the kale is soft. Season with salt.

. . . recipe continued

SERVES 2

Two 5 oz (155 g) haddock fillets

½ tsp (2.5 mL) salt

2 Tbsp (30 mL) vegetable oil

INDIAN SPICED BROTH

1 Tbsp (15 mL) olive oil

¼ tsp (1 mL) fennel seeds

2 Tbsp (30 mL) minced ginger

1 medium shallot, sliced

1 Tbsp (15 mL) minced garlic

½ tsp (2.5 mL) cumin

½ tsp (2.5 mL) allspice

Pinch of cloves

¼ tsp (1 mL) cardamon

¼ tsp (1 mL) salt

1 Tbsp (15 mL) sugar

3 cups (750 mL) beef broth

1 Tbsp (15 mL) unsalted butter

1 Tbsp (15 mL) chili oil

SPICED TOMATO CHUTNEY

1 cup (250 mL) diced beefsteak tomatoes

1 Tbsp (15 mL) minced ginger

1 tsp (5 mL) diced garlic

¼ tsp (1 mL) cinnamon

¼ tsp (1 mL) cumin

¼ cup (60 mL) sugar

¼ cup (60 mL) red wine vinegar

¼ tsp (1 mL) salt

. . . ingredients continued

. . . Pan-Seared Haddock in Indian Spiced Broth (continued)

ROASTED SHALLOTS

3 shallots

1 Tbsp (15 mL) vegetable oil

¼ tsp (5 mL) salt

BRAISED KALE

2 Tbsp (30 mL) unsalted butter

3 cups (750 mL) chopped kale

1 Tbsp (15 mL) diced ginger

¼ cup (60 mL) canned cannellini beans, drained

¼ tsp (1 mL) salt

GARNISH

Pea shoots

PAN-SEARED HADDOCK Season each piece of fish with ¼ tsp (1 mL) salt.

Heat 2 Tbsp (30 mL) vegetable oil in a pan over high heat. When the oil starts to smoke, add the fish and cook for 45 seconds, then place in the oven on the bottom rack for 3 minutes to finish cooking. The internal temperature should read 150°F (65°C). This will leave the fish cooked medium and tender in the middle.

Assembly

Divide the braised kale and beans into 2 serving bowls, then divide the roasted onions between them. Add the pan-seared haddock right in the centre of the bowl, top with the spiced tomato chutney, and gently pour the Indian spiced broth into the bowl. Garnish with pea shoots and enjoy.

Serve warm.

FISH TIP

Steaming gives fish a little boost of moisture, but remember, steam is very hot, so the cooking process will go fast. When opening the lid on your pot or steaming vessel, always open it away from your body, not toward you.

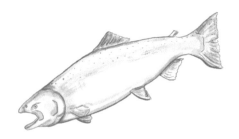

ANGLERS LUNCH

with Ramen Eggs / Quinoa Salad / Crunchy Vegetables /
Shiitake Mushroom Vinaigrette / Soft-Baked Salmon

SERVES 2

½ lb (250 g) salmon fillet

½ Tbsp (7.5 mL) vegetable oil

Pinch of salt

Cracked black pepper

RAMEN EGGS

2 free range eggs

1 cup (250 mL) soy sauce

1 Tbsp (15 mL) diced ginger

1 Tbsp (15 mL) diced garlic

**QUINOA SALAD AND
VEGETABLES**

½ cup (125 mL) cooked quinoa,
follow package instructions

¼ cup (60 mL) seeded and
diced cucumber

¼ cup (60 mL) diced tomato

⅓ cup (80 mL) edamame beans

2 cups (500 mL) spinach

**SHIITAKE MUSHROOM
VINAIGRETTE**

1 Tbsp (15 mL) vegetable oil

1 cup (250 mL) sliced
shiitake mushrooms

1 tsp (5 mL) minced ginger

1 tsp (5 mL) minced garlic

2 Tbsp (30 mL) soy sauce

1 Tbsp (15 mL) rice vinegar

½ tsp (2.5 mL) sesame oil

1 tsp (5 mL) honey

3 Tbsp (45 mL) grapeseed oil

This salad is packed with goodness for the mind, body, and soul, not to mention the flavour in the dressing, which is so good it's mind-altering. The shiitake mushroom dressing is soaked into the quinoa and makes for an amazing base with crunchy vegetables, soft-cooked salmon, and a protein-packed ramen egg. This is energy in a bowl!

This is great for a lunch on the go or even a dinner party! Plate it in a nice bowl for a dinner at home, or pack it in your favourite to-go packaging and enjoy it on the road, on a boat, or in the office . . .

"I finally know where superheroes get their powers from."

Method

RAMEN EGGS Add 4 cups (1 L) water to a pot and bring to a boil. With a sharp wooden skewer, gently grind a small hole in the bottom of each egg, just enough to pierce the shell. Add the eggs to the water and boil for 5 minutes and 45 seconds, then remove and place in an ice bath. Cool the eggs completely and remove the shells.

Place the peeled eggs into a coffee mug. Combine the soy sauce, ginger, and garlic in the mug and allow the eggs to marinate in the mixture for 2 hours in the fridge.

In anticipation of cooking the salmon, preheat oven to 300°F (150°C).

QUINOA SALAD AND VEGETABLES Place the cooked (and cooled) quinoa in a medium-size bowl and add all the vegetables. Toss gently, cover, and reserve.

SHIITAKE MUSHROOM VINAIGRETTE Add 1 Tbsp (15 mL) vegetable oil to a skillet over medium heat. Add the mushroom slices and sauté for 2 to 3 minutes until tender. In a bowl, combine the remaining shiitake mushroom vinaigrette ingredients together and add the warm mushrooms. Pour over the quinoa salad and toss to mix. This can be made in advance and stay in the fridge for a few days in an airtight container.

SOFT-BAKED SALMON Brush the salmon with ½ Tbsp (7.5 mL) vegetable oil and season with a pinch of salt and cracked black pepper. Place on a baking tray and bake in the oven for 15 to 20 minutes, until the internal temperature is about 150°F (65°C).

. . . recipe continued

Assembly

If you're packing this up for a fishing trip or lunch at the office, allow the salmon to cool completely before packing. Start with the quinoa salad and add the soft-baked salmon. Quick tip! Travel with the ramen eggs uncut, and when you're ready to eat them, cut with a knife or fishing line.

FISH TIP

This recipe works great with almost any fish—even canned salmon or tuna will work. If choosing canned salmon, I always use salmon that is wild and was processed somewhere close to me. Always look for options that tell you the species, such as wild sockeye salmon. I also look for a label telling me that the fish is ocean-friendly and a sustainable choice.

WARM LOBSTER POTATO SALAD

with Braised Bacon / Sun-Dried Tomato and Tarragon Vinaigrette /
Asparagus / Fingerling Potatoes

A salad doesn't always mean just a bowl of greens. This warm lobster salad with potatoes, bacon, and a dressing packed with flavours of tarragon, chewy sun-dried tomatoes, and olives is a knockout.

This salad makes for a great sharing dish. Plate it so each ingredient can shine, serve it proudly, and eat it with people ya love.

"This lobster salad is edible curiosity put into action."

Method

To cook your lobsters, boil a large pot of water over high heat. Place the lobster into the pot and cover with a lid. Cook the lobster for 5 minutes for the first 1 lb (450 g), and an additional 2 minutes per pound after that. Once cooked, immediately plunge the lobster into an ice bath for 10 minutes. After it has cooled, remove meat from the tail, claws, and knuckles. Save the shells and head for a soup or stock. For more info, see Fish Tip following the recipe.

Alternatively, if you don't want to cook live lobster, ask your fishmonger if you can pick up some freshly steamed lobster. They may even clean it up and separate the meat for you!

BRAISED BACON Preheat oven to 350°F (175°C).

Heat 1 tsp (5 mL) vegetable oil in a skillet over high heat. Add the bacon and sear on all sides until golden. Remove from heat and add the water, thyme, and garlic. Place a tight-fitting lid or aluminum foil over the skillet and place it in the oven. Cook the bacon for 1 hour, or until tender. Check the skillet halfway through the cooking process to see if it needs more water. Once the bacon is tender, keep warm for plating

SUN-DRIED TOMATO AND TARRAGON VINAIGRETTE Combine all the sun-dried tomato and tarragon vinaigrette ingredients in a large bowl and mix well. Reserve.

ASPARAGUS Simmer 2 cups (500 mL) water and the salt in a medium-size skillet. Blanch the asparagus spears for 1 minute, then remove from the water and immediately cool in an ice bath. Remove from the ice bath after 1 minute and reserve for plating.

. . . recipe continued

SERVES 2 TO 4

2 whole lobsters, cleaned

BRAISED BACON

1 tsp (5 mL) vegetable oil

5 oz (155 g) slab bacon, cut into 2-inch (5 cm) cubes

1 cup (250 mL) water

½ tsp (2.5 mL) dried thyme

2 cloves garlic, crushed

SUN-DRIED TOMATO AND TARRAGON VINAIGRETTE

1 small shallot, thinly sliced

¼ tsp (1 mL) minced garlic

1 tsp (5 mL) chopped tarragon

¼ cup (60 mL) chopped sun-dried tomatoes

3 Tbsp (45 mL) sherry vinegar

2 anchovies, finely chopped

¼ cup (60 mL) quartered Kalamata olives

¼ cup (60 mL) grapeseed oil

Pinch of salt

Pinch of white pepper

ASPARAGUS

1 tsp (5 mL) salt

5 to 10 cooked and cooled asparagus spears

FINGERLING POTATOES

1 tsp (5 mL) salt

4 large fingerling potatoes

GARNISH

½ cup (125 mL) arugula leaves

FINGERLING POTATOES Fill a pot with 4 cups (1 L) water and the salt. Lightly simmer then add the potatoes. Cook until fork tender, then remove the potatoes and allow them to cool slightly for about 5 minutes. Slice the potatoes in half and reserve.

Assembly

Spoon the potatoes onto a big white plate or platter. Cut the cooked lobster tails in half lengthwise and add to the salad followed by the knuckle pieces and whole claws. Add the vinaigrette and gently mix. Scatter around the cooked bacon, followed by the dressed lobster, and finish the plating by adding the asparagus and arugula leaves. Drizzle any remaining vinaigrette overtop.

FISH TIP

Try putting your lobsters in the freezer for about 30 minutes before cooking. They will go to sleep, and you will have little to no fuss when submerging them in boiling water. When cooking a whole lobster, have an ice bath ready. After the lobster is finished cooking, place it in the ice water—this will immediately stop the cooking process, making it easier to handle when cleaning. The lobster can be prepped ahead of time and simply warmed back up when you want to eat it. Remember to save the shells for a great bisque or stock.

TEX MEX-RUBBED HALIBUT TACO SALAD

with Rice and Beans / Santa Fe Salsa /
Cocoa Taco Sauce / Smashed Avocado

SERVES 2

Two 4 oz (125 g) halibut fillets

½ tsp (2.5 mL) salt

1 Tbsp (15 mL) olive oil

2 cups (500 mL) chopped iceberg lettuce

TEX-MEX RUB

½ tsp (2.5 mL) garlic powder

1 Tbsp (15 mL) chili powder

½ tsp (2.5 mL) cumin

½ tsp (2.5 mL) chili flakes

1 tsp (5 mL) oregano

RICE AND BEANS

½ cup (125 mL) jasmine rice

½ cup (125 mL) black beans

1 Tbsp (15 mL) unsalted butter

1 cup (250 mL) water

TACO BOWLS

4 cups (1 L) vegetable oil

Two 12-inch (30 cm) flour tortillas

¼ tsp (1 mL) salt

SANTA FE SALSA

1 cup (250 mL) seeded and diced
Roma tomatoes

⅓ cup (80 mL) canned corn kernels

⅓ cup (80 mL) diced red onion

1 Tbsp (15 mL) seeded and diced
jalapeño pepper

¼ tsp (1 mL) salt

1 tsp (5 mL) vegetable oil

. . . ingredients continued

As kids, my brother and I would come home from school, and I would usually have a salad for a snack. I've loved salads for as long I can remember, and this one is a rendition of a classic taco salad, but with a Spencer Watts twist: it features Tex Mex-style fish, a tangy cocoa taco sauce, rice, beans, and crispy lettuce. I could eat this salad anytime, day or night, and I hope it's the same for you.

This salad is the best because, guess what kids, you can eat the bowl. I use a large metal spoon to push the tortilla into a shallow bowl shape as it cooks. It's the perfect vessel for the salad.

"Inventor of the salad, smart! Inventor of the taco, smart! Inventor of the taco salad . . . genius!"

Method

TEX-MEX RUB Combine all the Tex-Mex rub ingredients in a small bowl and reserve.

RICE AND BEANS Combine the rice, beans, butter, water, and ½ tsp (2.5 mL) of the Tex-Mex rub in a saucepan with a tight-fitting lid. Cook over medium heat until all the water has been absorbed, about 10 to 15 minutes. Allow the rice to stand for 10 minutes. Remove the lid and gently fluff with a fork.

TACO BOWLS In a heavy-bottomed pot large enough to fit one 12-inch (30 cm) tortilla, heat 4 cups (1 L) vegetable oil until it reaches 375°C (190°C). Using a metal spoon or ladle, push the first flour tortilla into the hot oil to give it a bowl shape and hold it, submerged in oil, for 1 to 2 minutes, until it retains its shape. Continue to fry until the tortilla is golden and crispy. Remove carefully and place on a tray covered in kitchen towels to drain. Season with salt.

Repeat with the second tortilla.

SANTA FE SALSA Combine all the Santa Fe salsa ingredients in a small mixing bowl and reserve.

. . . recipe continued

COCOA TACO SAUCE

¼ cup (60 mL) taco sauce

½ tsp (2.5 mL) cocoa powder

SMASHED AVOCADO

1 ripe avocado

¼ tsp (1 mL) minced garlic

½ tsp (2.5 mL) lime juice

⅛ tsp (0.5 mL) chili flakes

⅛ tsp (0.5 mL) salt

GARNISH

Lime wedges

COCOA TACO SAUCE Mix the taco sauce and cocoa powder together with ½ tsp (2.5 mL) Tex-Mex rub and reserve.

SMASHED AVOCADO Add all the smashed avocado ingredients to a medium-size bowl and, with a whisk, lightly smash the avocado mixture up and down until it starts to get smooth. Whip the avocado mix vigorously until it's nice and creamy. Reserve for plating.

HALIBUT Heat the oven to 400°F (200°C). Season the top of each halibut fillet with ¼ tsp (1 mL) salt and ¼ tsp (1 mL) Tex-Mex rub. Heat 1 Tbsp (15 mL) olive oil in a skillet over high heat; add the halibut, seasoning side down, and sear for 45 seconds. Flip the fish with a spatula and place the skillet in the oven on the bottom rack. Cook 4 to 5 minutes. The internal temperature should come up to 145°F (63°C). This will leave the fish juicy in the centre.

Assembly

Fill each taco bowl with the chopped iceberg lettuce; add a scoop of rice and beans. Place the halibut alongside the rice and scatter the salsa around the fish and rice. Add a scoop of the smashed avocado and serve with the cocoa taco sauce and lime wedges on the side. Enjoy.

FISH TIP

Cooking fish with spice on it requires some attention. Although fish likes a good sear in a hot pan with a bit of oil, spices burn easily this way, and it can make them taste bitter instead of delicious. Season one side of the fish and cook it quickly for a short time, then flip it and finish cooking in a 400°F (200°C) oven.

"SMOKED" TROUT & SESAME SPINACH SALAD

with Sweet Sesame Dressing / Wasabi Popcorn

This salad is a rendition of a dish from a sushi restaurant my father and I used to go to behind a gas station in a bad part of town. The chef there had been cooking in that kitchen for 20 years or more, and even as a little boy I loved his food. We would sit at the sushi bar, and he would hand over this small, cold bowl of the most incredible salad made simply of salmon, dressing, and greens. It was perfect at the beginning of a meal or on its own for a light lunch. The restaurant is no longer there, and the chef has since retired, but in his honour I want to keep this little gem alive with an added twist—wasabi popcorn.

This little salad performs well with chopsticks in a small bowl or plate. I use little teacups and they work perfectly.

"It will only be over . . . if you stop."

Method

Preheat oven to 300°F (150°C).

SWEET SESAME DRESSING Combine all the sweet sesame dressing ingredients in a bowl and mix well. Set aside.

TROUT Place the fish on a baking tray covered in parchment paper. Brush the fish with ¼ tsp (1 mL) vegetable oil and liquid smoke and season with salt. Bake for 10 minutes.

WASABI POPCORN In a microwave-safe bowl, melt the butter along with the wasabi powder, and stir to combine. Add ½ Tbsp (7.5 mL) vegetable oil and the popcorn kernels to a saucepan over medium heat and cover with a lid. Keep the pot moving until the popcorn has popped, opening the lid slightly to let steam out every 5 to 10 seconds. When finished, toss the popcorn with the wasabi butter and sprinkle with salt.

Assembly

Remove the fish from the oven and allow to cool. Once cooled, flake the fish into the bowl with the dressing. Add the shredded spinach. Fold together and place in the serving bowls. Top with sesame seeds and wasabi popcorn.

. . . recipe continued

SERVES 2

Two 2½ oz (75 g) trout fillets

¼ tsp (1 mL) vegetable oil

¼ tsp (1 mL) liquid smoke

¼ tsp (1 mL) salt

1 cup (250 mL) shredded raw spinach

SWEET SESAME DRESSING

1 tsp (5 mL) soy sauce

1 Tbsp (15 mL) mayonnaise

½ tsp (2.5 mL) grated ginger

1 tsp (5 mL) tahini

1 tsp (5 mL) sugar

¼ tsp (1 mL) sesame oil

¼ tsp (1 mL) rice wine vinegar

WASABI POPCORN

1 tsp (5 mL) unsalted butter

¼ tsp (1 mL) wasabi powder

½ Tbsp (7.5 mL) vegetable oil

1 Tbsp (15 mL) popcorn kernels

Pinch of salt

GARNISH

Sesame seeds

FISH TIP

The best way to eat trout is without bones. If using a whole trout for this recipe, the bones are best removed after cooking. The back and rib bones (which are connected) can be easily removed, and you can discard any secondary bones that run through your fingers while flaking the cooked meat. If you want to debone the fish prior to cooking, I suggest butterflying the fish and pulling the backbone and "pin" bones out with fish tweezers.

HAND HELDS

A good burger, taco, or anything you can eat while holding it in your hands reminds me of
my big brother, Travis. Since we were kids, anytime we were at any sort of restaurant, on any occasion,
my brother would always get a "hand held" item—from burgers to lettuce wraps and even tacos.
This section is dedicated to my brother Travis. Love ya, Trav . . .

LOBSTER PUFFS 90

with Caramelized Onion and Anchovy Spread /
Puff Pastry / Garlic Butter Aioli

MAHI MAHI BAHN MI SUBMARINE 95

with XO Tomato Jam / Pickled Vegetables / Chili Mayonnaise

CRAB CAKE SLIDERS 98

with "Burger" Sauce / Garlic Butter Buns

JERK-RUBBED MAHI MAHI TACOS 103

with Quick Pickled Radish / Baja Slaw / Chipotle Remoulade

KOREAN CHILI-MARINATED SALMON LETTUCE WRAPS 106

with Pickled Cucumber / Spicy Sesame Buttermilk Drizzle / Crushed Peanuts

SESAME AND BLACK PEPPER-CRUSTED AHI TUNA BLT 111

with Wasabi Sesame Mayo / Crisp Bacon

SEA BASS & CHICKPEA FALAFEL WRAP 112

with Garlic Yogurt / Cucumber–Tomato Salsa / Spicy White Bean Hummus

PANKO-CRUSTED HALIBUT & SCALLOP "CHOP" BURGER 117

with Oven-Dried Tomatoes / Miracle Mayo

SMOKED SALMON, SALAMI, AND MORTADELLA MUFFULETTA SANDWICH 120

with Pickled Pepper Tapenade

NASHVILLE-STYLE CRISPY FRIED HALIBUT SANDWICH 125

with Pickle Chip Crust / Nashville Chili Oil / Dill Slaw

LOBSTER PUFFS

with Caramelized Onion and Anchovy Spread / Garlic Butter Aioli

SERVES 2 TO 4

6 oz (170 g) precooked lobster meat, finely diced

CARAMELIZED ONION AND ANCHOVY SPREAD

5 Tbsp (75 mL) olive oil, divided

2 Tbsp (30 mL) finely diced onion

2 cloves garlic, minced

2 Tbsp (30 mL) chopped fresh tarragon leaves

7 anchovy fillets

1 tsp (5 mL) salt

PUFF PASTRY

1 sheet puff pastry cut to 12 x 6 inches (30 x 15 cm), thawed

1 beaten egg, for egg wash, divided

GARLIC BUTTER AIOLI

2 Tbsp (30 mL) unsalted butter

1 clove minced garlic

½ cup (125 mL) mayo

2 Tbsp (30 mL) lemon juice

¼ tsp (1 mL) salt

GARNISH

Chives, sliced

Imagine a lobster roll but, instead of the classic roll, the lobster is piled onto a flavour-packed, puff pastry. The sweet, buttery lobster is perfect with the delicate, flaky pastry. Eating these always has me making sounds I didn't know I could make.

"Oh, Hank honey, look, they've got lobster. Let's get some."

Method

CARAMELIZED ONION AND ANCHOVY SPREAD Heat 1 Tbsp (15 mL) olive oil in a small pan over medium heat and add the diced onions. Cook for 5 minutes or until soft and lightly browned. Remove from heat and let cool.

In a food processor, combine the caramelized onions and minced garlic, tarragon, remaining oil, anchovy fillets, and salt. Pulse until well combined.

PUFF PASTRY Preheat oven to 375°F (190°C).

Take the puff pastry and cut to 12 × 6 inches (30 × 15 cm), making sure that the parchment paper is still underneath. Spread the caramelized onion and anchovy spread evenly over the sheet of puff pastry.

Using the parchment to help, roll the pastry over itself lengthwise, creating a rolled log. Brush the last 1 inch (2.5 cm) of the pastry with some of the egg wash to seal the roll, pressing the edges together. Put it in the freezer to firm up for 15 minutes.

Remove the log from the freezer and cut into ½-inch (1 cm) slices. Place those slices onto a parchment-lined baking tray and brush the puffs with the remaining egg wash. Bake in the preheated oven for 10 minutes. Remove from the oven and let cool to room temperature.

GARLIC BUTTER AIOLI Melt the butter in a small saucepan over medium heat. Add the minced garlic to the butter and let steep for 2 minutes.

Combine the rest of the garlic butter aioli ingredients in a mixing bowl, then slowly drizzle the butter overtop, whisking rapidly.

LOBSTER Add the diced lobster to a bowl and coat with the aioli.

. . . recipe continued

. . . Lobster Puffs (continued)

Assembly

Place the puffs on a long plate or platter and carefully spoon the lobster onto the puffs. Garnish with sliced chives and serve.

FISH TIP

When it comes to lobster, the sweetest meat comes from the freshest source. Cooking live lobster at home is the best option, but if that is out of your comfort zone you can purchase frozen raw lobster meat, which makes it easier to handle when cooking.

Here I am in my mid-twenties on the edge of the Fraser River in BC for the sockeye run. I am scraping the back bone out of a freshly caught salmon that I am going to use in some ravioli. You can see my big silver hoop earrings, my chain wallet, and my metal skull belt buckle . . . I miss those shoes.

MAHI MAHI BANH MI SUBMARINE

with XO Tomato Jam / Pickled Vegetables / Chili Mayonnaise

The banh mi is here! Leave it to the French and Vietnamese to invent the perfect tag team for food culture. The result is this one-of-a-kind sandwich, and mine features fresh grilled mahi mahi on a crispy French baguette, packed with pickled vegetables, chili mayo, and sweet and sour tomato jam that is bursting with umami. This sandwich is so good it hurts.

I serve this sandwich on a rectangle plate with extra chili mayo on the side.

"Hey Tommy . . . I'll trade you my dessert for your sandwich . . . Not a chance, Dennis."

Method

Preheat oven to 400°C (200°C).

XO TOMATO JAM Toss the dried shrimp, shallots, garlic, ginger, and chilies into a food processor and blend to a coarse paste. Place a medium saucepan over medium-high heat and add ⅓ cup (80 mL) vegetable oil. Once the oil is hot, fry the diced prosciutto for 2 minutes. Add the shrimp and vegetable mix and cook until the prosciutto is golden and crisp and the vegetables are dark in colour. Add the tomatoes and cook for an additional 4 to 5 minutes. Add the soy sauce, rice wine vinegar, sugar, and oyster sauce and cook until jammy. Remove from heat and allow to cool. XO should be thick and have a jam-like texture with a layer of oil on top.

PICKLED VEGETABLES Combine the cucumber and carrot in a bowl. In a separate bowl, mix together the vinegar, sugar, salt, and water, then pour over the vegetables and allow to marinate. Cover and refrigerate.

CHILI MAYONNAISE Combine all the chili mayonnaise ingredients in a bowl and reserve.

MAHI MAHI Make sure the mahi mahi is patted dry. Season the fish with ¼ tsp (1 mL) each salt and pepper. In a large skillet over high heat, add 1 Tbsp (15 mL) olive oil. When the oil is smoking, add the fish, seasoning side down. Sear for 45 seconds, flip, and cook the fish in the oven for 2 to 5 minutes. The internal temperature should read 140°F (60°C) when cooked to medium rare, so that it is tender and juicy in the middle.

SERVES 2

Two 4 oz (125 g) mahi mahi portions

¼ tsp (1 mL) salt

¼ tsp (1 mL) pepper

1 Tbsp (15 mL) olive oil

1 baguette, cut in half lengthwise, pointed ends removed

½ cup (125 mL) cilantro

XO TOMATO JAM

1 Tbsp (15 mL) dried shrimp

2 medium shallots, chopped

2 Tbsp (30 mL) chopped garlic

2 Tbsp (30 mL) chopped ginger

2 Tbsp (30 mL) sliced fresh chilies

⅓ cup (80 mL) vegetable oil

⅓ cup (80 mL) diced prosciutto

1 cup (250 mL) diced cherry tomatoes

2 Tbsp (30 mL) soy sauce

1 Tbsp (15 mL) rice wine vinegar

1 Tbsp (15 mL) sugar

1 Tbsp (15 mL) oyster sauce

PICKLED VEGETABLES

Half an English cucumber, shredded

1 medium carrot, shredded

2 Tbsp (30 mL) rice wine vinegar

1 Tbsp (15 mL) sugar

Pinch of salt

1 Tbsp (15 mL) water

. . . ingredients continued

. . . recipe continued

Assembly

CHILI MAYONNAISE

⅓ cup (80 mL) mayonnaise

1 Tbsp (15 mL) chili oil

1 tsp (5 mL) sugar

1 tsp (5 mL) lime juice

¼ tsp (1 mL) fish sauce

Spread the chili mayonnaise on the inside of the cut baguette (both on the top and bottom) and place the pickled vegetables on the bottom with the fresh cilantro. Add the seared mahi mahi and dress the fish with the XO jam. Cut into 2 sandwiches and enjoy.

FISH TIP

Mahi mahi is a lean fish with great flavour. To make sure I get a nice even cook, I like to bring the mahi mahi up to room temperature (about 10 minutes) before cooking it. It cooks faster and more evenly for mahi mahi and most other fish.

CRAB CAKE SLIDERS

with "Burger" Sauce / Garlic Butter Buns

SERVES 2 TO 4

½ lb (250 g) crab meat

3 Tbsp (45 mL) vegetable oil

CRAB CAKES

2 Tbsp (30 mL) mayonnaise

2 Tbsp (30 mL) panko breadcrumbs

¼ tsp (1 mL) salt

¼ tsp (1 mL) pepper

½ tsp (2.5 mL) steak spice

½ tsp (2.5 mL) Worcestershire sauce

1 tsp (5 mL) lemon zest

1 Tbsp (15 mL) diced jalapeño

"BURGER" SAUCE

1 Tbsp (15 mL) ketchup

½ cup (125 mL) mayonnaise

1 Tbsp (15 mL) chopped capers

1 Tbsp (15 mL) Dijon mustard

¼ tsp (1 mL) paprika

¼ tsp (1 mL) vinegar

½ tsp (2.5 mL) sugar

GARLIC BUTTER BUNS

1 tsp (5 mL) minced garlic

¼ tsp (1 mL) salt

¼ tsp (1 mL) pepper

¼ cup (60 mL) unsalted butter, softened

4 slider buns

The slider was invented in the 1940s by Naval officers. The ship's galley cooked and served small greasy burgers that would "slide right down." The rest, as they say, is history. My sliders are a little different. I am not 80 miles off the Pacific coast, wondering why I joined the Navy and how I ended up with the nickname "Shark Bait." These sliders are super fun and the crab cake rocks! The sauce is my version of a not-so-classic drive-in burger mayo, and I like to brush garlic butter on the buns for an added layer of flavour. It's heaven.

These sliders look really good plated on a long platter or wood board. Line them up like little soldiers and serve them with lots of napkins.

"Sun's out, buns out, baby!"

Method

Preheat oven to 375°F (190°C).

CRAB CAKES Flake through the crab meat to ensure that there are no stray pieces of shell.

Combine all the crab cake ingredients in a bowl, pressing the mixture down firmly and covering in plastic wrap. Place in the fridge for 30 minutes to set.

"BURGER" SAUCE Combine all the burger sauce ingredients in a bowl and mix well. Reserve.

GARLIC BUTTER BUNS Mix the garlic, salt, and pepper together with the butter and brush on the buns.

Remove the crab mixture from the fridge and form into 4 equal-size patties. Place 3 Tbsp (45 mL) vegetable oil in a skillet over medium-high heat. Place the crab cakes into the hot oil and fry for 1 minute. Flip the burgers, then place the pan in the oven for 2 to 3 minutes until golden brown and warmed through.

While the crab cakes are in the oven, place the garlic butter buns, cut side down, in a hot skillet and gently toast them.

Serve the crab cakes on the garlic butter buns with the burger sauce on insides of the bun. Enjoy!

. . . recipe continued

. . . Crab Cake Sliders (continued)

FISH TIP

When using frozen crab, I look for rock crab or Dungeness crab mix. If you can't find that product, you can use fresh crab. Use the same weight and remember, when using frozen crab, make sure to completely defrost, and always squeeze out excess moisture. Check for and discard shell bits.

JERK-RUBBED MAHI MAHI TACOS

with Quick Pickled Radish / Baja Slaw / Chipotle Remoulade

Heat wave! This is my island in the sun . . . oiy oiy. Tacos are on and the blender needs another frozen concoction! These tacos are so good, make sure you only invite the people you really like. The warm spice notes of the jerk rub go so well with the meaty mahi mahi, and with a perfectly crunchy slaw and chipotle remoulade—aka supercharged tartar sauce—this fish taco is dressed and ready to impress.

Great tip coming at ya: When I make fish tacos, I make lots of them, and a taco holder is the way to go. You can find them at most kitchen shops, and they work wonders. You can also turn a muffin tin upside down, which works as well.

"If you haven't heard a rumour by 9:30 . . . start one."

Method

Preheat oven to 375°F (190°C).

JERK RUB Mix all the jerk rub ingredients together in a small bowl until well combined. Set aside.

QUICK PICKLED RADISH Combine the quick pickled radish ingredients in a small jar or resealable container with a lid, shake well, and keep cool.

BAJA SLAW Combine all the Baja slaw ingredients, except for the cabbage, in a medium-sized bowl and mix well. Add the cabbage and toss to coat with the dressing. Set aside.

CHIPOTLE REMOULADE Combine the chipotle remoulade ingredients together in a small bowl and mix well. Set aside.

MAHI MAHI Season the fish on both sides with the jerk rub.

Add 1 Tbsp (15 mL) vegetable oil to a pan over medium-high heat. Sear the fish for 20 seconds and flip with a spatula. Place the fish in the oven and cook for 3 to 5 minutes. The internal temperature should read 150°F (65°C). The fish will be juicy in the middle. Flake the fish into strips with a spatula.

. . . recipe continued

SERVES 2 TO 4

Two 5 oz (155 g) mahi mahi fillets

1 Tbsp (15 mL) vegetable oil

6 to 8 small tortillas, warmed in a skillet or microwave

JERK RUB

1 tsp (5 mL) chili powder

1 tsp (5 mL) cayenne

1 Tbsp (15 mL) brown sugar

1 Tbsp (15 mL) allspice

¼ tsp (1 mL) cloves

¼ tsp (1 mL) cinnamon

¼ tsp (1 mL) nutmeg

1 tsp (5 mL) garlic powder

QUICK PICKLED RADISH

1 cup (250 mL) thinly sliced radish

⅓ cup (80 mL) red wine vinegar

2 Tbsp (30 mL) sugar

BAJA SLAW

2 Tbsp (30 mL) mayonnaise

1 tsp (5 mL) sugar

1 tsp (5 mL) white vinegar

¼ tsp (1 mL) dill

1 tsp (5 mL) grainy Dijon mustard

¼ tsp (1 mL) salt

1 cup (250 mL) shredded green cabbage

1 cup (250 mL) shredded red cabbage

. . . ingredients continued

Assembly

CHIPOTLE REMOULADE

1 Tbsp (15 mL) diced shallots

1 Tbsp (15 mL) diced chipotle peppers

1 tsp (5 mL) whole capers

½ cup (125 mL) mayonnaise

2 tsp (10 mL) lemon juice

¼ tsp (1 mL) salt

GARNISH

Lime wedges

Jalapeño slices

Cilantro

Line a taco holder with the warmed tortillas. Fill each with the Baja slaw, then add strips of mahi mahi and top with the chipotle remoulade. Garnish with the pickled radish, lime, jalapeño slices, and cilantro. Enjoy.

FISH TIP

The mahi mahi "bone" line runs down the centre of the fish (the dark line). This part needs to be removed. Run your knife down each side of the bone line and discard, leaving two clean loins to cut portions from.

KOREAN CHILI-MARINATED SALMON LETTUCE WRAPS

with Pickled Cucumber / Spicy Sesame Buttermilk Drizzle /
Crushed Peanuts

SERVES 2 TO 4

12 oz (340 g) Atlantic salmon,
centre-cut fillet

2 cups (500 mL) uncooked
jasmine rice

2 heads butter lettuce

KOREAN BBQ MARINADE

⅓ cup (80 mL) gochujang Korean
chili paste or Thai chili sauce

1 tsp (5 mL) minced ginger

1 tsp (5 mL) minced garlic

½ tsp (2.5 mL) sesame oil

1 Tbsp (15 mL) sesame seeds

1 Tbsp (15 mL) honey

½ Tbsp (7.5 mL) water

1 tsp (5 mL) soy sauce

PICKLED CUCUMBER

1 cup (250 mL) sliced cucumber

½ cup (125 mL) rice wine vinegar

1 Tbsp + 1 tsp (20 mL) sugar

¼ tsp (1 mL) salt

¼ tsp (1 mL) allspice

. . . ingredients continued

This dish is the flavour grenade of food in every sense. The fatty salmon takes on every ounce of flavour from the Korean BBQ glaze, and the love affair between the BBQ salmon and the pickled cucumber is something out of one of my grandmother's romance novels. Drizzle on some spicy sesame buttermilk for an extra kick and these lettuce wraps are going to be showing up weekly.

Lettuce wraps are in the building! These are super fun because you can "build your own bite" right at the table, or they can be pre-plated for what I like to call "hand-bombs," whether you're entertaining or making them for a quick bite. They work great served on a big platter.

"Sometimes the smallest bites have the biggest flavour."

Method

Preheat oven to 400°F (200°C).

Cook the jasmine rice according to the package instructions while preparing the recipe.

KOREAN BBQ MARINADE Combine all the Korean BBQ marinade ingredients together in a small mixing bowl and mix well. Set aside.

SALMON Place the salmon on a parchment-lined baking tray. Paint with two-thirds of the Korean BBQ marinade (reserve the remaining third to serve on the side). Bake for 15 to 20 minutes. The salmon should be cooked medium, with an internal temperature of about 150°F (65°C). This will leave the salmon tender and juicy in the middle.

PICKLED CUCUMBER Combine all the pickled cucumber ingredients in a bowl and let soak in the vinegar for 10 minutes.

SPICY SESAME BUTTERMILK DRIZZLE Combine all the spicy sesame buttermilk drizzle ingredients and mix well. Set aside.

. . . recipe continued

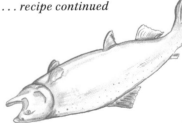

Assembly

I serve the salmon right on the parchment. Organize the garnishes around it in small eclectic bowls, along with the rice. Serve with lettuce leaves to wrap the salmon in.

FISH TIP

Any time I purchase salmon fillets, I always remove the bellies, vacuum pack them, and freeze. These make the perfect appetizer in a pinch—they are super fatty, defrost in minutes, and cook ultra-quick.

If you want to get even more crafty, you can marinate the bellies then freeze, upping the flavour and making a big splash in no time.

SPICY SESAME BUTTERMILK DRIZZLE

1 Tbsp (15 mL) buttermilk

⅓ cup (80 mL) mayonnaise

½ tsp (2.5 mL) minced garlic

1 tsp (5 mL) sesame oil

1 tsp (5 mL) rice wine vinegar

½ tsp (2.5 mL) sugar

¼ tsp (1 mL) cayenne pepper

¼ tsp (1 mL) salt

GARNISH

¼ cup (60 mL) crushed peanuts

¼ cup (60 mL) sliced red chilies

¼ cup (60 mL) sliced green onion

SESAME AND BLACK PEPPER-CRUSTED AHI TUNA BLT

with Wasabi Sesame Mayo / Crispy Bacon

A club sandwich is all about texture and flavour, and ahi tuna is dense and melt-in-your-mouth delicious. It loves creamy mayo and crunchy sesame seeds and bacon . . . okay, everything loves bacon, but tuna is no exception! My version introduces some fun Asian flavours into the traditional club and the result is like fireworks in July: an explosion of taste and texture.

"The all-new BLT: bacon, lettuce, and tuna. Now available for a limited time."

Method

WASABI SESAME MAYO Combine all the wasabi sesame mayo ingredients in a bowl and mix well. Set side.

CRUSTED TUNA Toast the sesame seeds in a dry frying pan over medium, moving the pan every few seconds. Toast until fragrant.

Spread the sesame seeds on a flat plate. Add the salt and pepper. Press each piece of tuna into the seeds and coat the outside of the fish on both sides.

Heat 1 Tbsp (15 mL) vegetable oil in a frying pan over high heat and sear the tuna on each side for 30 to 45 seconds.

Assembly

Toast 6 slices of brioche bread and spread each with wasabi sesame mayo. Place lettuce and tomato on 4 mayo-covered slices of bread, season each tomato with salt and pepper, and top with tuna and bacon. You should now have 4 open-faced sandwiches and 2 pieces of mayo-spread toast. Place the sandwiches on top of each other, then top with the slices of toast, mayo side down, for a total of two 2-tiered sandwiches (see photo for a reference). Serve with potato chips and dig in!

FISH TIP

When I purchase canned tuna, I always look for the MSC label, which stands for Marine Stewardship Council. This has been recognized as an ocean-friendly seafood choice. This tuna is guilt-free and good for the soul.

SERVES 2

Two 5 oz (155 g) ahi tuna steaks, halved horizontally

6 slices of brioche bread

4 lettuce leaf ends

8 thin slices Roma tomato

8 slices cooked bacon

Salt, to taste

Pepper, to taste

Sea salt potato chips, for serving

WASABI SESAME MAYO

⅓ cup (80 mL) mayonnaise

1 tsp (5 mL) wasabi

½ tsp (2.5 mL) sesame oil

½ tsp (2.5 mL) lime juice

¼ tsp (1 mL) salt

¼ tsp (1 mL) pepper

CRUSTED TUNA

2 Tbsp (30 mL) black sesame seeds

2 Tbsp (30 mL) white sesame seeds

½ tsp (2.5 mL) salt

1 tsp (5 mL) pepper

1 Tbsp (15 mL) vegetable oil

SEA BASS & CHICKPEA FALAFEL WRAP

with Garlic Yogurt / Cucumber–Tomato Salsa /
Spicy White Bean Hummus

6 oz (170 g) sea bass fillet, cut into large cubes

3 cups (750 mL) vegetable oil

2 tortilla wraps, large

2 cups (500 mL) shredded Romaine

GARLIC YOGURT

½ cup (125 mL) plain Greek yogurt

¼ tsp (1 mL) cumin

½ tsp (2.5 mL) minced garlic

2 tsp (10 mL) lemon juice

¼ tsp (1 mL) salt

2 Tbsp (30 mL) water

CUCUMBER–TOMATO SALSA

¼ cup (60 mL) diced cucumber

½ cup (125 mL) diced Roma tomatoes

¼ cup (60 mL) diced red onion

1 Tbsp (15 mL) olive oil

¼ tsp (1 mL) allspice

¼ tsp (1 mL) salt

1 Tbsp (15 mL) chopped mint leaves

1 tsp (5 mL) lemon juice

. . . ingredients continued

Loaded for impact, this wrap may knock you off your feet. Sea bass is the perfect fish to pair with Middle Eastern spices, and with the texture of the chickpeas, you'll never look at falafels the same way again. Add garlic yogurt and creamy spicy hummus, and this hand held will leave you saying, "That's a wrap!"

These wraps are great for lunch, dinner, or a picnic. If you're travelling, you can wrap them up in parchment paper or cut and serve them on a big platter. Either way, bring napkins!

"Sea bass falafel—it's everything you want it to be and more."

Method

Heat 3 cups (750 mL) vegetable oil in a heavy-bottomed pot until it reaches 375°F (190°C).

GARLIC YOGURT Combine all the garlic yogurt ingredients in a bowl and mix well. Cover and place in the fridge until ready to use.

CUCUMBER–TOMATO SALSA Add the diced cucumber, tomatoes, and red onion to a bowl. Add the olive oil, allspice, salt, mint, and lemon juice. Stir gently to combine. Set aside until ready to use.

SPICY WHITE BEAN HUMMUS Combine the navy beans, garlic, hot sauce, lemon juice, and salt in a mini food processor. Start to blitz and add the oil in a stream, until thick and creamy. Set aside until ready to use.

SEA BASS & CHICKPEA FALAFEL Combine the sea bass, 3 Tbsp (45 mL) olive oil, chickpeas, garlic, parsley, cumin, lemon zest, allspice, cilantro, salt, and pepper in a food processor and blitz until a coarse paste is achieved. Divide and shape the mixture into eight 1 to 1½ oz (30 to 45 g) balls and set on a parchment-lined tray. Deep-fry in preheated oil a few at a time for 2 minutes or until golden brown. Remove from the oil and let rest on a plate lined with kitchen towels.

Repeat until all the falafels are cooked.

. . . recipe continued

Assembly

Lay down your tortillas and spread liberally with white bean hummus. Add the lettuce and 4 falafels per tortilla.

Top with cucumber–tomato salsa and drizzle with garlic yogurt, hot sauce, and sprouts. Enjoy!

FISH TIP

If you do not have a food processor, you can always hand-cut the sea bass, but make sure the fish has been completely patted dry. First, cut in thin strips lengthwise, then group a few strips together and thinly slice into small cubes. This will give you the perfect size to build into a falafel.

SPICY WHITE BEAN HUMMUS

1 cup (250 mL) canned navy beans, drained

1 tsp (5 mL) minced garlic

1 tsp (5 mL) hot sauce

1 Tbsp (15 mL) lemon juice

¼ tsp (1 mL) salt

3 Tbsp (45 mL) olive oil

SEA BASS & CHICKPEA FALAFEL

3 Tbsp (45 mL) olive oil

½ cup (125 mL) canned chickpeas, drained

1 tsp (5 mL) chopped garlic

¼ cup (60 mL) parsley

¼ tsp (1 mL) cumin

1 Tbsp (15 mL) lemon zest

¼ tsp (1 mL) allspice

¼ cup (60 mL) cilantro

¼ tsp (1 mL) salt

¼ tsp (1 mL) pepper

GARNISH

Hot sauce

Sprouts

PANKO-CRUSTED HALIBUT & SCALLOP "CHOP" BURGER

with Oven-Dried Tomatoes / Miracle Mayo

Chop burgers are always great, but this one has seafood royalty: fresh halibut and scallops. These two seafood friends make the ideal textured burger. Panko breadcrumbs give this burger the perfect crunch, and with tangy mayo, crisp lettuce, and oven-dried tomatoes, it's a home run.

I serve this burger proudly. Whether it's on your favourite china or a disposable plate, this burger holds its own.

"I feel like Babe Ruth standing at home plate, pointing to the bleachers, knowing I am about to make history."

Method

Preheat oven to 400°F (200°C).

OVEN-DRIED TOMATOES Place the tomato slices onto a parchment-lined baking tray. Combine the olive oil, salt, thyme, and sugar, and sprinkle over the tomatoes. Bake for 35 minutes until soft.

MIRACLE MAYO Whisk all the miracle mayo ingredients together and reserve for plating.

CHOP BURGER PATTIES Combine the halibut, scallops, panko, mayonnaise, lemon zest, tarragon, seafood seasoning, salt, and pepper in the bowl of a full-size food processor and pulse to a coarse paste. If you are using a small food processor, I recommend doing this in two parts to avoid overfilling the mixer. Place the seafood mixture into a bowl, press down, and cover with plastic wrap. Place in the fridge for 20 minutes to firm up.

Heat 4 cups (1 L) vegetable oil in a heavy-bottomed pot over medium to medium-high heat until it reaches 350°F (175°C). Form the burger mix into 2 equal patties. Make each patty slightly bigger than the bun.

. . . recipe continued

SERVES 2

5 oz (155 g) halibut, diced

5 oz (155 g) scallops, diced

4 brioche burger buns

Torn iceberg lettuce

French fries, for serving

Ketchup, for serving

OVEN-DRIED TOMATOES

1 beefsteak tomato, cut into 4 slices

1 Tbsp (15 mL) olive oil

¼ tsp (1 mL) salt

¼ tsp (1 mL) dried thyme

¼ tsp (1 mL) sugar

MIRACLE MAYO

¼ cup (60 mL) mayonnaise

½ tsp (2.5 mL) malt vinegar

¼ tsp (1 mL) garlic powder

¼ tsp (1 mL) mustard powder

¼ tsp (1 mL) sugar

Pinch of salt

CHOP BURGER PATTIES

2 Tbsp (30 mL) panko breadcrumbs

2½ Tbsp (37 mL) mayonnaise

1 tsp (5 mL) lemon zest

1 tsp (5 mL) tarragon

¼ tsp (1 mL) seafood seasoning

½ tsp (2.5 mL) salt

½ tsp (2.5 mL) pepper

4 cups (1 L) vegetable oil

. . . ingredients continued

BREADING

2 eggs

½ cup (125 mL) all-purpose flour

1 cup (250 mL) panko breadcrumbs

BREADING Crack the eggs into a bowl and whisk. Add the flour to a second bowl, and the panko to a third. Dip each burger patty in flour, then egg, then panko. Place both patties into the hot oil for 2 to 3 minutes until golden brown. Remove and drain on a kitchen towel–lined tray.

Assembly

Spread the miracle mayo on the insides of each bun. Place the iceberg lettuce on the bottom buns. Place the oven-dried tomatoes on top of the burger patties, then place the patties on the iceberg lettuce and add the top buns. Serve with french fries and ketchup. Enjoy!

FISH TIP

To bind chop burgers, there are a few tips. First, make sure the fish chunks are small, as smaller pieces bind together better than bigger pieces. I bind my burger with a bit of mayonnaise. You can also make a mousse by adding egg whites and a touch of cream to the raw fish, then adding seasoning when you blitz the seafood into a paste. This along with breadcrumbs makes the perfect binder for the burger, giving it a super seafood taste.

SMOKED SALMON, SALAMI, AND MORTADELLA MUFFULETTA SANDWICH

with Pickled Pepper Tapenade

1 wide, round, flat loaf of bread

Olive oil as needed

6½ oz (185 g) mortadella

2 oz (60 g) salami

6½ oz (185 g) smoked salmon lox

4 slices Provolone cheese

4 slices Swiss cheese

Pepperoncini peppers, for serving

PICKLED PEPPER TAPENADE

1 cup (250 mL) green olives with pimento

1 tsp (5 mL) crushed garlic

3 anchovy fillets

⅓ cup (80 mL) chopped Peppadew peppers (or your favourite pickled pepper)

⅓ cup (80 mL) parsley

2 Tbsp (30 mL) olive oil

¼ tsp (1 mL) pepper

A proper deli sandwich can blow your hair back and leave you in a state of bliss. This muffuletta is no exception. I love this sandwich because it can be made in no time. Once the tapenade is made, the rest is just good quality ingredients, some great soft bread, and you're set!

This is the ideal sandwich for a picnic or game day. It can be made ahead of time, wrapped in plastic, and carted anywhere. Regardless of where you are, this sandwich needs to be in your life.

"A sandwich should be crafted like the finest watch, every element working together in a perfect symphony."

Method

PICKLED PEPPER TAPENADE Combine all the pickled pepper tapenade ingredients in a mini food processor and pulse until a coarse paste is achieved. Set aside until ready to serve.

Assembly

Cut the loaf of bread in half horizontally. Spread half the pickled pepper tapenade on the bottom of the loaf and half on the top. Generously drizzle both pieces with olive oil. Place half of your mortadella onto the tapenade-covered bottom piece of bread and top with half the salami slices and half the smoked salmon. Add all 8 slices of cheese. Add the remaining salmon slices, then the salami, then the mortadella. Place the second half of the bread on top. Wrap the sandwich tightly in plastic wrap and place in the fridge for 2 hours. Remove and cut the sandwich into 4 wedges. Serve with pepperoncini peppers.

. . . recipe continued

I had just woken up from a nap. Two fish were caught while I was sleeping and I was clearly unimpressed.

. . . Smoked Salmon, Salami, and Mortadella Muffuletta Sandwich (continued)

FISH TIP

When you only use a few anchovies from your tin and want to save the rest for another recipe, remove them from the tin and put them in a small mason jar or canning jar with a lid. Cover the anchovies with a good quality oil and refrigerate. This will preserve the anchovies and season the oil.

NASHVILLE-STYLE CRISPY FRIED HALIBUT SANDWICH

with Pickle Chip Crust / Nashville Chili Oil / Dill Slaw

This sandwich is bad to the bone and crazy good. The halibut is the perfect meaty texture to be fried like the Colonel's chicken, and once dredged through spices and chili oil, the halibut gets a new identity. The dill pickle potato chip crust gives the halibut unbelievable crunch, and the spice is quickly cooled off with fresh crunchy slaw. The pickles give the whole experience attitude.

This sandwich is unapologetically delicious and mind-bendingly satisfying. Serve it with a box of baby wipes and an ice-cold beer.

"Hair back, elbows out, hunch over and brace for impact!"

Method

BUTTERMILK MARINADE Combine all the buttermilk marinade ingredients in a bowl and add the portioned halibut. Cover and refrigerate.

PICKLED CHIP DREDGE Combine the flour, potato chips, and pepper in a baking dish and set aside.

NASHVILLE CHILI OIL Combine the dry spices together in a bowl. Reserve ¼ cup (60 mL) of the spice mix to sprinkle on the cooked halibut.

Heat ½ cup (125 mL) grapeseed oil in a pot over medium heat. Add the remainder of the dry spice mix and whisk in. Allow it to steep on low heat for 10 minutes, stirring every few minutes.

Strain the mixture through a cheesecloth into a clean bowl and set aside.

DILL SLAW Combine the mayonnaise, vinegar, dill, sugar, salt, and pepper and mix well. Toss with the cabbage until well coated. Set aside until ready to assemble.

. . . *recipe continued*

SERVES 2

Two 4 oz (125 g) halibut fillets

4 cups (1 L) vegetable oil

2 brioche burger buns

Mayonnaise, to taste

1 dill pickle, sliced + extra dill pickles for serving on the side

Dill pickle potato chips

BUTTERMILK MARINADE

1 cup (250 mL) buttermilk

1 egg

1 Tbsp (15 mL) pickle brine

PICKLED CHIP DREDGE

1 cup (250 mL) all-purpose flour

1 cup (250 mL) crushed dill pickle potato chips

¼ tsp (1 mL) pepper

NASHVILLE CHILI OIL

½ tsp (2.5 mL) cayenne

1 Tbsp (15 mL) sugar

2 Tbsp (30 mL) chili powder

1 tsp (5 mL) garlic powder

1 tsp (5 mL) onion powder

1 Tbsp (15 mL) smoked paprika

1 Tbsp (15 mL) sweet paprika

¼ tsp (1 mL) salt

½ cup (125 mL) grapeseed oil

. . . *ingredients continued*

DILL SLAW

1 Tbsp (15 mL) mayonnaise

½ tsp (2.5 mL) white vinegar

½ tsp (2.5 mL) dill

½ tsp (2.5 mL) sugar

Pinch of salt

Pinch of pepper

1 cup (250 mL) packed
shredded cabbage

FISH Heat 4 cups (1 L) vegetable oil in a heavy-bottomed pot to 350°F (180°C).

Remove the halibut from the buttermilk marinade, allowing any excess marinade to fall off. Place the fish in the dredge and pack it. Put the fish back into the marinade then back again into the dredge (this is known as the "double dredge," resulting in a super crunchy coating).

Gently lower both coated pieces of fish into the hot oil and cook for 4 to 5 minutes. Remove and place on a baking sheet lined with kitchen towels.

Baste and brush heavily with the Nashville chili oil and finish with a light dusting of the reserved dry spice mix.

Assembly

Spread the insides of each brioche bun with mayonnaise. Add the crunchy dill slaw and some sliced dill pickles. Place the halibut on top and close with the top bun.

Serve with dill pickle potato chips and dill pickles.

FISH TIP

Using the escalope* cut on the halibut is perfect for this sandwich. This allows more surface area for the crunchy coating, plus the fish cooks quicker and sits on the bun evenly, giving the perfect fish-to-bun ratio. It's science!

*Escalope: A French term meaning "very thin."

CHAPTER NO. 4
PASTA, NOODLES, AND DOUGH

This section is full of drool-worthy recipes, featuring everything that's basically
in the "cheat day" category, and that's totally fine with me! From spicy noodles to pasta
stuffed with seafood, this chapter is off the hook.

PORK & SHRIMP DAN DAN NOODLES 130

with Spinach / Szechuan Pepper Sauce

RED HOT SHRIMP "SAUSAGE" LINGUINI 133

with Spicy Italian Tomato Sauce / Basil Parmesan Cream

PAN-SEARED SCALLOPS WITH SQUID INK PASTA 136

with Oven-Roasted Tomatoes / Parsley Gremolata

ROASTED BLACK COD PAPPARDELLE 141

with Leeks / Spring Pea Purée / Sage Cream / Fried Sage Leaves

ATLANTIC CANDIED SALMON & SPINACH CANNELLONI 144

with Vegetable Caponata / Hollandaise Sauce

DRUNKEN LOBSTER NOODLES 149

with Spicy "Drunken" Sauce / Thai Basil

ANCHOVY & CARAMELIZED ONION TART 150

with Sun-Dried Tomatoes / Kalamata Olives

PARISIENNE GNOCCHI AND SLOW-ROASTED LING COD 153

with Spiced Green Apple Chutney / Saffron Butter Sauce / Savoy Cabbage

SALT COD PHYLLO PIE 156

with Whipped Potato Filling / Lemon–Parsley Pesto / Feta Cheese

BUTTER CRAB SAMOSA 161

with Cumin Potatoes / Peshwari Dough / Cilantro Chutney / Tamarind Dip

PORK & SHRIMP DAN DAN NOODLES

with Szechuan Pepper Sauce / Spinach

SERVES 2 TO 4

½ lb (250 g) ground pork

5 oz (155 g) shrimp, peeled and deveined (see Fish Tip, page 201), diced

MARINADE

1 Tbsp (15 mL) vegetable oil

1 Tbsp (15 mL) minced garlic

1 tsp (5 mL) chopped ginger

1 Tbsp (15 mL) dark soy sauce

⅛ tsp (0.5 mL) crushed Szechuan pepper

SZECHUAN PEPPER SAUCE

¼ cup (60 mL) tahini paste

1 Tbsp (15 mL) dark soy sauce

1½ Tbsp (22 mL) sugar

½ Tbsp (7.5 mL) chili oil

½ Tbsp (7.5 mL) crushed Szechuan pepper

SPINACH

1 Tbsp (15 mL) sesame oil

1 tsp (5 mL) diced ginger

3 cups (750 mL) spinach

1 Tbsp (15 mL) sesame seeds

¼ tsp (1 mL) salt

UDON NOODLES

½ lb (250 g) udon noodles

¼ tsp (1 mL) salt

GARNISH

Green onions, sliced

Peanuts, crushed

Sesame seeds

Dan dan noodles have entered the building! This Szechuan specialty is street food at its finest. The shrimp and pork work in perfect harmony, along with lots of spinach, udon noodles, and tingly Szechuan pepper.

I serve these noodles in a small, deep bowl. It's perfect for constantly mixing and playing with the noodles, the way dan dan should be eaten.

"Playing with your food. Perfectly acceptable."

Method

MARINADE Break up the pork into a bowl. Add the diced shrimp and all the marinade ingredients and mix together. Cover and marinate for 10 minutes.

Heat 1 Tbsp (15 mL) vegetable oil in a frying pan over medium-high heat. Fry the pork and shrimp until crisp and cooked through. Reserve in the pan.

SZECHUAN PEPPER SAUCE In a separate bowl, whisk all the Szechuan pepper sauce ingredients together until smooth, then add to the pork and shrimp mix. Cook until hot and thick (1 minute). Reserve for plating.

SPINACH Heat 1 Tbsp (15 mL) sesame oil with the ginger in a pan over medium-high heat. Add the spinach, sesame seeds, and salt, and turn over several times to wilt. Once wilted, drain on a tray lined with kitchen towels. Reserve for plating.

UDON NOODLES Place the udon noodles in boiling salted water for 3 minutes. Drain.

Assembly

Place the spinach in the bottom of the bowls. Top with the hot udon noodles, then the pork and shrimp sauce mixture. Garnish with green onions, crushed peanuts, and sesame seeds.

FISH TIP

If I am not using local fresh shrimp, I always look for frozen ASC shrimp. This is the Aquaculture Stewardship Council logo, which denotes that the shrimp have been farmed in a sustainable and environmentally sensitive way. Perfect for your family, the planet, and dan dan noodles!

RED HOT SHRIMP "SAUSAGE" LINGUINI

with Spicy Italian Tomato Sauce / Basil Parmesan Cream

Pasta should have simple, humble ingredients and, when put together correctly, leave you speechless. This pasta is so simple but so effective. The spicy tomato sauce gets its flavour from the shrimp shells and naturally sweet tomatoes. The thick sauce is perfect for linguini noodles, and once nestled into pesto cream, this pasta checks off all the boxes.

I serve this pasta twisted high to the sky in my favourite coupe bowl. *"When I eat this pasta, I'm usually wearing a 'Do Not Disturb' sign."*

Method

SPICY ITALIAN TOMATO SAUCE Heat 1 Tbsp (15 mL) olive oil in a skillet over medium-high. Add the onion and garlic and sauté for 1 minute. Add the shrimp shells and cook for another 45 seconds. Add the chili flakes and salt. Stir. Add the cherry tomatoes and cook for another 5 to 10 minutes, or until the cherry tomatoes are cooked. Deglaze the pan with the white wine and reduce until the wine is almost evaporated. Add the tomato paste and cook for another 2 minutes, then add the crushed tomatoes. Reduce the sauce for 5 minutes. Strain the sauce through a fine mesh sieve and keep warm over low heat.

GROUND SHRIMP MIXTURE Place all the ground shrimp mixture ingredients, except for the oil, into a mini chopper or food processor and pulse until you have a coarse "sausage like" consistency. Heat 1 Tbsp (15 mL) olive oil in a medium-size saucepan over medium heat. Add the shrimp mixture and sauté for 1 minute. Set aside.

BASIL PARMESAN CREAM Combine all the basil Parmesan cream ingredients except for the whipping cream in a mini blender and blitz to a coarse paste. Pour the whipping cream into a pan over medium heat and reduce for 2 minutes. Add the basil purée to the whipping cream and cook until the sauce can coat the back of a spoon. Reserve for plating.

PASTA Cook the pasta in a pot of salted boiling water, according to package instructions, until al dente.

Add the strained Italian tomato sauce to the ground shrimp mixture, then add the cooked linguini and mix well.

. . . recipe continued

SERVES 2

½ lb (250 g) shrimp, shells removed and reserved, deveined (see Fish Tip, page 201)

4 oz (125 g) linguine noodles

SPICY ITALIAN TOMATO SAUCE

1 Tbsp (15 mL) olive oil

1 cup (250 mL) diced onion

1 Tbsp (15 mL) minced garlic

1 tsp (5 mL) chili flakes

½ tsp (2.5 mL) salt

1 cup (250 mL) halved cherry tomatoes

½ cup (125 mL) white wine

2 Tbsp (30 mL) tomato paste

3 cups (750 mL) canned crushed tomatoes

GROUND SHRIMP MIXTURE

¼ tsp (1 mL) cayenne

½ tsp (2.5 mL) fennel seeds

1 tsp (5 mL) chopped garlic

¼ tsp (1 mL) salt

1 Tbsp (15 mL) olive oil

BASIL PARMESAN CREAM

½ cup (125 mL) packed fresh basil

1 Tbsp (15 mL) pine nuts

¼ cup (60 mL) grated Parmesan cheese

1 tsp (5 mL) minced garlic

1 Tbsp (15 mL) olive oil

¼ tsp (1 mL) salt

½ cup (125 mL) whipping cream

. . . ingredients continued

Assembly

GARNISH

Parmesan cheese, shaved

Chili flakes

Sprouts

Chili oil

Pool the basil Parmesan cream in the bottom of each bowl. Add the linguini by twisting and lowering the pasta onto the bowl. Garnish with grated Parmesan, chili flakes, sprouts, and, for an extra kick, a spoonful of chili oil. Enjoy!

FISH TIP

To make the shrimp mixture you can pulse the shrimp lightly in a food processor or chop by hand. Either way, make sure the shrimp resembles a coarse paste; this will feel like ground sausage and cook up very quickly, while taking on flavour.

PAN-SEARED SCALLOPS AND SQUID INK PASTA

with Oven-Roasted Tomatoes / Parsley Gremolata

SERVES 4

8 to 12 scallops, depending on the size

1 lb (450 g) linguini noodles (squid ink looks great, if you can find it)

Salt, to taste

1 cup (250 mL) lemon soy butter (see page 198 and double the recipe)

1 Tbsp (15 mL) vegetable oil

2 Tbsp (30 mL) unsalted butter, for basting

OVEN-ROASTED TOMATOES

½ cup (125 mL) cherry tomatoes

1 Tbsp (15 mL) olive oil

½ tsp (2.5 mL) salt

½ tsp (2.5 mL) pepper

PARSLEY GREMOLATA

1 tsp (5 mL) unsalted butter

½ cup (125 mL) panko breadcrumbs

1 Tbsp (15 mL) chopped parsley

¼ tsp (1 mL) minced garlic

1 Tbsp (15 mL) lemon zest

Pinch of salt

GARNISH

Parmesan cheese, shaved

There is a delicate wow factor in this scallop and squid ink pasta and that's okay. The lemon soy butter makes for the perfect pasta sauce and complements the scallops like I compliment my mom when she gets her hair done. The cherry tomatoes give it the perfect touch of sweetness, and the gremolata gives it just the right amount of crunch.

"Scallops and lemon soy butter . . . we're trending."

Method

OVEN-ROASTED TOMATOES Toss the cherry tomatoes with the olive oil, salt, and pepper. Place on a baking tray and roast in a 400°F (200°C) oven for 10 minutes, or until the tomatoes start to blister and soften.

PARSLEY GREMOLATA Melt the butter in a medium-size skillet over medium-high heat. Once the butter has melted, add the remaining parsley gremolata ingredients. Continuously stir until the mixture is golden brown and fragrant. Remove from heat and reserve.

LINGUINI Cook the linguini in boiling salted water for 7 minutes or until tender. Remove, drain, and add to the lemon soy butter sauce; mix to combine. Keep warm.

SCALLOPS Pat the scallops dry on a piece of kitchen towel and season with salt.

Heat 1 Tbsp (15 mL) olive oil in a frying pan over medium heat. Once the oil starts to ripple and slightly smoke, carefully place the scallops into the pan flat side down. After cooking for about 1 minute, flip the scallops over and cook for another minute. Try not to touch the scallops other than when flipping. After the scallops have cooked on each side, turn off the heat and add 2 Tbsp (30 mL) butter to the hot pan. Using a spoon, baste the scallops with the melted butter for 1 minute. Remove the scallops from the pan.

. . . recipe continued

Assembly

With a pair of tongs, twist the linguini onto a plate. Place the scallops and oven-roasted tomatoes around the pasta. Garnish the scallops with parsley gremolata and finish with shaved Parmesan peels.

FISH TIP

When cooking frozen scallops, slack thaw them in the fridge overnight, and be sure to pat them dry completely before pan-searing in a very hot pan.

ROASTED BLACK COD PAPPARDELLE

with Leeks / Spring Pea Purée / Sage Cream / Fried Sage Leaves

This pasta has the attitude of a hunter's dinner. The buttery leeks and sage cream are the perfect supporting roles for the fatty fish. With crunchy hazelnuts and a bright green purée, this recipe provides a whole new outlook on pasta.

I serve this pasta on a large plate or in a shallow bowl. The noodles are so thick they pile up easily, creating the perfect mountain to dig into.

"This pasta makes me look way better than I am."

Method

HAZELNUTS Preheat oven to 245°F (120°C). Place ½ cup (125 mL) hazelnuts on a baking sheet and toast for 45 minutes. Discard the skins with a kitchen towel and crush the hazelnuts. Set aside.

Increase oven temperature to 400°F (200°C) for the cod.

LEEKS Melt the butter in a frying pan over low to medium heat. Add the leeks, salt, and thyme; let them cook slowly until softened. Set aside until ready to serve.

SPRING PEA PURÉE Add all the spring pea purée ingredients to a pot and cook over medium-low heat until warmed through. Purée with a blender (or immersion blender) until smooth. This recipe yields extra pea purée that you can save in the fridge for another day.

SAGE CREAM Place the pancetta in a skillet and sauté until crispy. Add the garlic and shallot; cook for 1 minute while stirring. Add the chopped sage and white wine and reduce until the wine has evaporated. Add the fish stock and reduce for 1 minute. Add the whipping cream and lemon juice and season with salt and white pepper. Reduce until the sauce can coat the back of a spoon.

PAPPARDELLE NOODLES Cook the pappardelle noodles in a large pot of boiling salted water, according to the package instructions, until al dente.

. . . recipe continued

SERVES 2

Two 5 oz (155 g) black cod fillets, skin on

½ cup (125 mL) hazelnuts

5 pappardelle nests

½ tsp (2.5 mL) salt

1 Tbsp (15 mL) vegetable oil

LEEKS

3 Tbsp (45 mL) unsalted butter

1 cup (250 mL) washed and sliced leeks

¼ tsp (1 mL) salt

¼ tsp (1 mL) dried thyme

SPRING PEA PURÉE

½ medium shallot, sliced

1⅓ cups (330 mL) frozen peas

1 Tbsp (15 mL) unsalted butter

½ tsp (2.5 mL) salt

½ tsp (2.5 mL) pepper

⅓ cup (80 mL) water

SAGE CREAM

⅓ cup (80 mL) finely diced pancetta

1 tsp (5 mL) minced garlic

1 medium shallot, thinly sliced

¼ cup (60 mL) chopped fresh sage

⅓ cup (80 mL) white wine

⅓ cup (80 mL) fish stock

1½ cups (375 mL) whipping cream

1 tsp (5 mL) lemon juice

¼ tsp (1 mL) salt

¼ tsp (1 mL) white pepper

. . . ingredients continued

FRIED SAGE LEAVES

⅓ cup (80 mL) vegetable oil

10 sage leaves (approx.)

GARNISH

Parmesan cheese, shaved

FRIED SAGE LEAVES Heat ⅓ cup (80 mL) vegetable oil in a skillet over medium heat. Add the sage leaves and fry for about 30 seconds, until they start to crackle and turn dark green. Dry on a kitchen towel.

BLACK COD Season the fish skin with ¼ tsp (1 mL) salt per fillet. Heat 1 Tbsp (15 mL) vegetable oil in a skillet over high heat. Once the oil is smoking, place the fish in the pan, skin side down, and press lightly with a spatula to sear the skin, about 20 seconds.

Place the pan with the fish in the 400°F (200°C) oven for 5 minutes, or until the internal temperature of the fish reaches 145°F (63°C). This will result in a flaky piece of fish that is tender throughout.

Assembly

Toss the pappardelle noodles in the warm sage cream with the cooked leeks.

Swirl a big spoonful of spring pea purée around the serving bowl. Place the sauced pappardelle noodles into the bowl and top with the toasted hazelnuts. Add the seared black cod and garnish with fried sage leaves and Parmesan cheese. Enjoy!

FISH TIP

Black cod is very fatty, so it's super nice and tender when it cooks. It's more expensive than other cod, but very hard to overcook due to the fat content. It's the perfect cut if you're new to cooking fish. I leave the skin on, which helps keep the flesh intact during the cooking process.

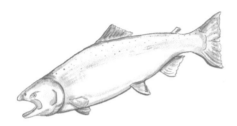

ATLANTIC CANDIED SALMON & SPINACH CANNELLONI

with Vegetable Caponata / Hollandaise Sauce

SERVES 4

Two ½ lb (250 g) centre-cut
Atlantic salmon loins (4 × 7 inch/
10 × 18 cm pieces)

4 oven-ready lasagna sheets

MARINADE

1 cup (250 mL) brown sugar

1 Tbsp + 1 tsp (20 mL) soy sauce

VEGETABLE CAPONATA

1 Tbsp (15 mL) vegetable oil

1 cup (250 mL) diced onion

1 Tbsp (15 mL) minced garlic

1 cup (250 mL) diced eggplant

1 cup (250 mL) diced zucchini

½ cup (125 mL) canned
crushed tomatoes

¼ tsp (1 mL) dried thyme

¼ tsp (1 mL) salt

¼ tsp (1 mL) pepper

SPINACH

2 Tbsp (30 mL) unsalted butter

1 tsp (5 mL) diced garlic

5 cups (1.25 L) spinach

¼ tsp (1 mL) salt

. . . ingredients continued

Candied salmon and cannelloni finally get hitched. This recipe is full of flavour and wow factor.

Using store-bought lasagna sheets makes for easy work. The candied salmon is something my dad has been making for years, but wrapped up in a pasta bundle with hollandaise, sautéed spinach, and an incredibly charismatic vegetable caponata, this dish is outrageously good.

This can be served two ways: family style in the dish it was cooked in, or in individual servings. If you are going to plate it individually, put the caponata veg on top of the cannelloni and the garnish. If it's family style, fill the cooking dish with the caponata then the cannelloni. Bake and serve the sauce on the side.

"I wish I had a time machine so I could go back and tell myself about this recipe sooner."

Method

MARINADE Mix the brown sugar and soy sauce into a paste. Place the salmon in a tight-fitting container and brush the soy and sugar paste onto the salmon. Cover and let marinate in the fridge for 2 to 4 hours. (The brown sugar and soy mix should have the texture of wet cement. Once it marinates, the sugars break down and turn into a liquid marinade over the course of a few hours.)

VEGETABLE CAPONATA Heat 1 Tbsp (15 mL) vegetable oil over medium-high; add the onion and garlic and sauté for a minute. Add the remaining vegetables and seasonings and reduce for 5 minutes. Lower heat and simmer until thick.

SPINACH Heat 2 Tbsp (30 mL) butter in a frying pan over medium heat and add the garlic. Add the spinach and sauté until wilted. Season with salt and rest the spinach on a tray lined with kitchen towels.

. . . recipe continued

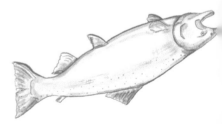

HOLLANDAISE SAUCE Place the egg yolks, lemon juice, salt, sugar, hot sauce, and wine into a blender. Start the blender and add the melted butter slowly as the mixture blends. If the sauce is too thick, add a small amount of water. Keep warm for plating. Always remember, hollandaise has a 4 hour window. After 4 hours, discard any leftover sauce.

LASAGNA Blanch the lasagna sheets in salted boiling water until 90% cooked. Remove and place on a parchment-lined baking sheet.

CANNELLONI Preheat oven to 375°F (190°C). Remove the salmon from the marinade, remove any excess marinade, and pat dry.

Place a piece of salmon on top of each lasagna sheet. Top with spinach and roll the pasta around the salmon and spinach until the edges meet. Cut off the excess pasta. Cover the tray with aluminum foil and bake for 20 minutes. The internal temperature of the salmon should reach 150°F (65°C).

HOLLANDAISE SAUCE

4 egg yolks

1 Tbsp (15 mL) lemon juice

¼ tsp (1 mL) salt

¼ tsp (1 mL) sugar

¼ tsp (1 mL) hot sauce

2 Tbsp (30 mL) white wine

½ cup (125 mL) melted unsalted butter

Water

GARNISH

Pea shoots

FISH TIP

When I cut the salmon for the cannelloni, I cut the fillet lengthwise. This fits the pasta sheet almost perfectly. Remember to cut nice thick loins. This will give you more evenly cooked fish when you're baking the cannelloni.

DRUNKEN LOBSTER NOODLES

with Spicy "Drunken" Sauce / Thai Basil

Drunken noodles have nothing to do with alcohol. Actually . . . there usually is alcohol involved, but not in this dish. These noodles could very well be my last meal ever, they are that good. The flat rice noodles are perfect because they cling to the delicious spicy, dark soy sauce. Finished with Thai basil, these noodles are quick, super tasty, and addictive.

Drunken noodles need to be served in a deep bowl, piping hot and spicy! Don't forget the chopsticks.

"Warning: These noodles may become addictive."

Method

NOODLES Fill a metal bowl with 12 cups (3 L) hot tap water. Place the noodles in the warm water and allow them to sit for 30 minutes or until soft. Drain and reserve.

SPICY "DRUNKEN" SAUCE Mix all the spicy "drunken" sauce ingredients together in a bowl and set aside.

STIR-FRY Heat a wok over medium-high heat. Add the oil, garlic, and sesame seeds. Cook for 30 seconds. Add the sauce and noodles and stir-fry for 1 minute while constantly tossing and folding. Add the lobster and toss to coat. Keep the food moving to heat through quickly. Finish with the green onion and Thai basil.

Assembly

Divide into bowls and serve hot. Enjoy!

FISH TIP

Lobster can be purchased in a few different varieties:

FRESH LOBSTER: The fishmonger can usually cook this for you and clean it as well, which saves time.

FROZEN TAILS: This option works great if tackling a whole lobster seems intimidating.

CLEANED FROZEN: "Knuckles." This is literally no-hassle lobster. There are no shells, which means no work for you. Just defrost if needed and follow the recipe.

SERVES 2 TO 4

5 oz (155 g) precooked lobster (see Fish Tip following recipe), cubed

½ lb (250 g) rice noodles

SPICY "DRUNKEN" SAUCE

2 Tbsp (30 mL) oyster sauce

2 Tbsp (30 mL) dark soy sauce

1 Tbsp (15 mL) light soy sauce

1 Tbsp (15 mL) Sriracha sauce

1 Tbsp (15 mL) minced garlic

1 Tbsp (15 mL) minced ginger

1 Tbsp (15 mL) sliced shallots

2 Tbsp (30 mL) brown sugar

¼ tsp (1 mL) fish sauce

1 Tbsp (15 mL) water

1 Tbsp (15 mL) sesame seeds

STIR-FRY

1 Tbsp (15 mL) vegetable oil

1 Tbsp (15 mL) diced garlic

1 Tbsp (15 mL) toasted sesame seeds

2 Tbsp (30 mL) sliced green onion

½ cup (125 mL) chopped Thai basil leaves

GARNISH

Green onions, sliced

Sesame seeds

ANCHOVY & CARAMELIZED ONION TART

with Sun-Dried Tomatoes / Kalamata Olives

SERVES 4 TO 5

Half a 2 oz (56 g) tin
of anchovies

One 9-inch (23 cm) store-bought
pastry crust

¼ cup (60 mL) sun-dried tomatoes

¼ cup (60 mL) pitted and halved
Kalamata olives

CARAMELIZED ONIONS

2 Tbsp (30 mL) vegetable oil

6 medium Spanish onions,
thinly sliced

¼ tsp (1 mL) salt

¼ tsp (1 mL) pepper

½ tsp (2.5 mL) chopped
fresh thyme

GARNISH

Fresh thyme leaves

This tart is as simple as it gets and super easy to make. Using store-bought pastry makes this one a no-brainer. The anchovies and caramelized onions are the perfect match of salty and sweet. The salty kick of the anchovy is slapped right in the face by the natural sweetness and deep flavour of the caramelized onions. The sun-dried tomatoes are chewy and tart, and the olives bring everything together in this French-inspired tart. If you are a fan of salt, buttery pastry, and show-stopping goodness, this is a must try.

For the tart, you can cut it up and serve it family style, or present it as a whole and wow the entire squad.

"I said, 'No thanks' when I should have said, 'Heck Yeah!'"

Method

CARAMELIZED ONIONS Heat 2 Tbsp (30 mL) vegetable oil in a frying pan over low to medium heat. Add the sliced onions and toss to coat. Cook for 45 to 60 minutes until soft, sweet, and caramelized. Season with salt, pepper, and thyme.

TART Preheat oven to 375°F (190°C). Fill the pie crust with the onions and lightly press them down. Bake in the oven for 20 minutes or until the pastry is fully cooked and crispy.

Assembly

Remove the pie from the oven and carefully place the anchovies in lines across the top of the onions. Place the roasted red peppers in lines across the anchovies to make a grid pattern. Place the halved olives face down in the squares created by the grid. Garnish with thyme and serve warm.

FISH TIP

When I cook with anchovies, I always use the ones packed in oil. I think they have the perfect amount of saltiness, and the extra oil leaves them nice and juicy. Don't be afraid if you get a little bit of that oil on the tart. #umami

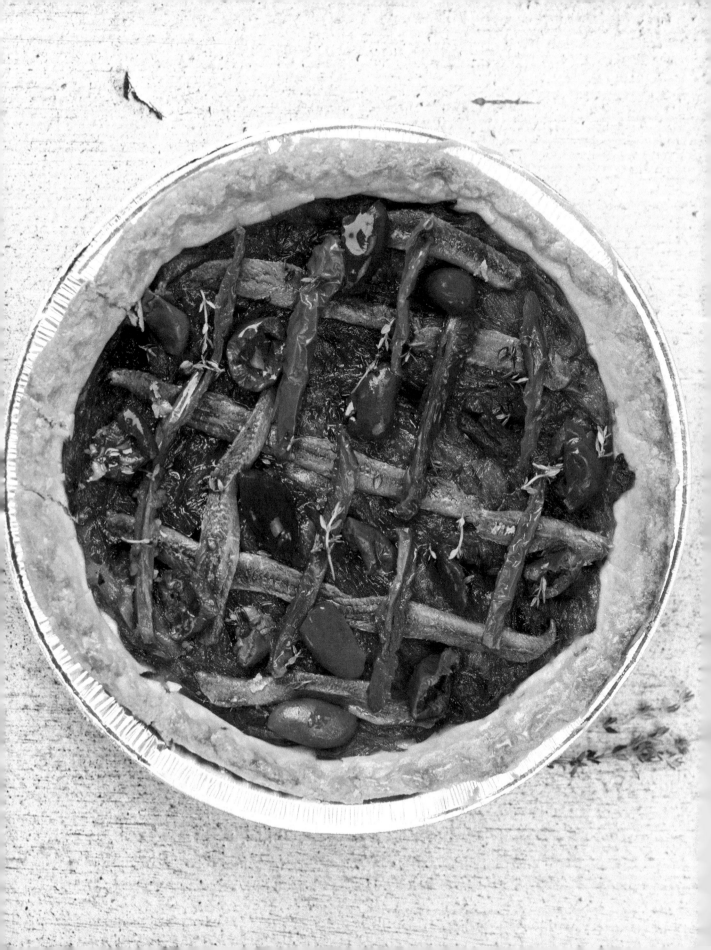

PARISIENNE GNOCCHI AND SLOW-ROASTED LING COD

with Spiced Green Apple Chutney / Saffron Butter Sauce / Savoy Cabbage

Okay, I know what you're thinking . . . can I really save 10% on my car insurance by switching to Geico? Totally kidding. This one looks crazy, but in reality it's super approachable. The pillowy gnocchi and spiced apple chutney can be made ahead of time, and the creamy butter sauce can be prepared and hot-held until you're ready to plate. When it comes time to eat, simply sauté the cabbage, roast the fish, and, while the fish is cooking, warm the gnocchi. This dish packs so much flavour, showcases great technique, and will wow those lucky enough to be at your table for dinner!

This is a hearty dish that sits nicely on an oval platter for family style dining. It's also an extremely stunning dish plated individually. I use a plain bowl and let the ingredients sing—black or white, the contrast between the white fish and yellow butter sauce on top of a black bowl makes this dish fun and inviting.

"But wait, there's more! Operators are standing by and we want to double your order."

Method

PARISIENNE GNOCCHI Tie a piece of butcher's twine to the two handles of a large pot filled with water (see Fish Tip following recipe). Season the water with salt and bring to a rapid simmer.

Warm the milk and butter in a pot over medium heat. Add the Dijon mustard and lemon juice and stir. Once the butter has melted, add the flour and stir until a paste forms. Transfer the paste to a stand mixer with the paddle attachment. Add an egg and beat until well incorporated and the mix becomes smooth. Repeat with the other eggs, one at a time. Add the salt and pepper and whip the mixture until creamy.

Place the mixture into a piping bag. Using the butcher twine as a cutting aid, pipe bite-size 1-inch (2.5 cm) pillows of the dough into the boiling water. Allow the dough to cook for a few minutes. Once it starts to float, give it another 90 seconds to cook in the boiling water, then remove to a lightly oiled baking tray. Allow to rest until ready to reheat and serve.

. . . recipe continued

SERVES 2

Two 6 oz (170 g) ling cod fillets

1 Tbsp (15 mL) olive oil

Pinch of kosher salt

3 Tbsp (45 mL) unsalted butter, for reheating the gnocchi

PARISIENNE GNOCCHI

⅔ cup + 5 Tbsp (235 mL) milk

⅓ cup + 1 tsp (85 mL) unsalted butter

1 Tbsp (15 mL) Dijon mustard

1 Tbsp (15 mL) lemon juice

1 cup (250 mL) all-purpose flour

3 eggs

¼ tsp (1 mL) salt

¼ tsp (1 mL) pepper

SPICED GREEN APPLE CHUTNEY

2 green apples, peeled, finely diced

3 Tbsp (45 mL) brown sugar

1 Tbsp (15 mL) apple cider vinegar

2 Tbsp (30 mL) unsalted butter

⅛ tsp (0.5 mL) cardamom

. . . ingredients continued

SAFFRON BUTTER SAUCE

2 Tbsp (30 mL) chopped shallots

¼ tsp (1 mL) saffron

¼ cup (60 mL) white vinegar

¼ cup (60 mL) white wine

¼ tsp (1 mL) dried thyme

1 tsp (5 mL) minced garlic

⅓ cup (80 mL) whipping cream

½ cup (125 mL) unsalted butter, cubed and chilled

¼ tsp (1 mL) salt

SAVOY CABBAGE

2 Tbsp (30 mL) unsalted butter

3 cups (750 mL) shredded savoy cabbage

1 Tbsp (15 mL) water

¼ tsp (1 mL) salt

GARNISH

Pea shoots

SPECIAL EQUIPMENT

Piping bag with a large round tip

SPICED GREEN APPLE CHUTNEY Combine the apples, brown sugar, apple cider vinegar, butter, and cardamom in a small pot over medium-low heat and reduce until thick and jammy.

SAFFRON BUTTER SAUCE Mix the shallots, saffron, vinegar, white wine, thyme, and garlic together in a pot over medium heat and reduce until almost dry. Add the whipping cream and bring to a simmer. Reduce the cream by half. Whisk in cold cubes of butter, one piece at a time, and melt while continuously moving the pan. Season with salt, then strain into a clean pot and keep warm until ready to serve.

SAVOY CABBAGE Melt the butter in a large skillet over medium heat. Add the cabbage and toss to coat. Add the water and salt and cover with a lid to cook until softened.

LING COD Preheat oven to 380°F (193°C). Cover a baking tray with parchment paper and lightly oil and salt the fish. Bake in the oven for 6 minutes, until flaky. The internal temperature should read 145°F (63°C); the fish will be cooked medium and tender in the middle.

Assembly

Reheat the gnocchi by adding 3 Tbsp (45 mL) water and 3 Tbsp (45 mL) butter to a skillet over medium heat and whisking them continuously until the butter has melted. Add the gnocchi and gently simmer until warmed through, swirling the pan every 30 to 45 seconds.

Add a pool of saffron butter sauce to the base of 2 plates. Add the warmed gnocchi and scatter the cooked savoy cabbage around the gnocchi. Place the ling cod in the middle of the gnocchi and add scoops of the green apple chutney. Garnish with pea shoots and enjoy!

When oven-roasting fish, you want the oven at the perfect temperature, with enough heat to get the fish crisp but not so much that it overcooks and burns it. I find 380°F (193°C) is perfect for a thick-cut piece of cod simply brushed with oil and seasoned with salt.

When cooking your gnocchi, try tying butcher twine across the pot onto each handle, which works as your "cutting" tool to make the perfect shapes. Once the gnocchi float, remove them from the water. Remember, the water should be at a light simmer while cooking.

SALT COD PHYLLO PIE

with Whipped Potato Filling / Lemon–Parsley Pesto / Feta Cheese

12 oz (340 g) salt cod

1 pkg (1 lb/454 g) phyllo
pastry, thawed

¼ cup (60 mL) melted unsalted
butter, for brushing the pastry

WHIPPED POTATO FILLING

⅓ cup (80 mL) milk

½ cup (125 mL) unsalted butter

¼ tsp (1 mL) pepper

1 tsp (5 mL) diced garlic

2 medium russet potatoes,
peeled and cubed

LEMON–PARSLEY PESTO

1 cup (250 mL) parsley

1 tsp (5 mL) chopped garlic

1 Tbsp (15 mL) lemon zest

¼ tsp (1 mL) salt

3 Tbsp (45 mL) olive oil

¼ cup (60 mL) pine nuts

GARNISH

Feta cheese

SPECIAL EQUIPMENT

Piping bag

Eating this dish is like getting full access to a secret club—anyone who eats it feels special and you never want it to end.

Calling the pastry crispy is an understatement, and with the saltiness of the cod filling and the bright flavours of lemon and herbs, this phyllo pie has it all when it comes to texture and flavour. The desalting process for the fish takes 24 hours, but I promise good things come to those who wait. It's designed as a community dish, so cut it at the table and let everyone be a part of that crunch experience.

"We asked if this pie was crispy. You said no, and the lie detector test determined that was a lie."

Method

SALT COD Rinse the salt cod under cold water for 90 seconds, rubbing off any excess surface salt. Cut the cod into large pieces and place them in a glass container filled with cold water for 24 hours. Change the water every 6 to 8 hours as it soaks. Discard the water after each soak.

WHIPPED POTATO FILLING Add the milk, butter, pepper, garlic, and salt cod pieces to a pot over medium heat. Lightly simmer until fully cooked, about 2 to 3 minutes.

Cook the peeled potatoes in simmering water unit extremely soft. Strain the potatoes thoroughly then add them back to the pot they were cooked in. Using a whisk, mash the potatoes using an up and down motion until you have a sand-like texture.

Strain the milk used to cook the cod into the bowl with the potatoes. Whisk and whip for 30 to 45 seconds until smooth. Flake the salt cod into the potatoes and whip again. Set aside.

LEMON–PARSLEY PESTO Combine all the lemon–parsley pesto ingredients together and place in a food processor/chopper. Blitz to combine.

... recipe continued

Assembly

Preheat oven to 375°F (190°C).

In a tart pan, place a sheet of phyllo on the bottom. Add 3 slightly askew sheets of phyllo on top of the first, covering the bottom and building the pastry up the sides of the pan. Brush the pastry with melted butter. Repeat with another 2 sheets of phyllo, brushing each with butter.

Fill a large piping bag with the whipped potato filling and cut the tip opening to the size of a quarter.

See opposite page for a step-by-step demonstration of how to build the pie: Starting in the middle of the pie, pipe a spiral pattern with about a ½-inch (13 mm) gap between the circles. Take 3 sheets of phyllo and stick them together, end to end; crinkle the phyllo lengthwise. Starting from the middle of the pie, fill the gaps between the potato spiral with the phyllo until you have a pastry spiral and the gaps are all filled.

Add dollops of the lemon–parsley pesto around the whipped potato filling and brush the top generously with butter. Bake for 35 to 45 minutes until the crust is golden brown.

Sprinkle with feta cheese and serve warm.

FISH TIP

When poaching fish, remember not to "boil" the poaching liquid. Poaching works best at a very low simmer, allowing the fish to soak up lots of flavour in the poaching liquid. A slower cook also decreases the likelihood of overcooking the fish.

BUTTER CRAB SAMOSA

with Cumin Potatoes / Peshwari Dough /
Cilantro Chutney / Tamarind Dip

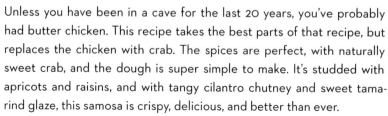

Unless you have been in a cave for the last 20 years, you've probably had butter chicken. This recipe takes the best parts of that recipe, but replaces the chicken with crab. The spices are perfect, with naturally sweet crab, and the dough is super simple to make. It's studded with apricots and raisins, and with tangy cilantro chutney and sweet tamarind glaze, this samosa is crispy, delicious, and better than ever.

I serve these many different ways, but I always like to make the presentation fun and worthy of a picture.

"You don't have to be a magician to make these disappear."

Method

CUMIN POTATOES Simmer 3 cups (750 mL) water in a pot and add the potatoes. Cook until fork tender, then drain. Combine the potatoes in a small mixing bowl with the vegetable oil, cumin, and salt and mix well. Allow to cool to room temperature before filling the samosas.

PESHWARI DOUGH Using a food processor, combine the flour, butter, raisins, apricots, salt, pepper, and sugar, pulsing until you achieve a sand-like consistency. Place the mixture into a bowl and add ¼ cup (60 mL) water. Knead the mixture to combine. Cover and let rest in the fridge for 30 minutes.

CILANTRO CHUTNEY Add the cilantro, ginger, lemon juice, and salt to a food processor and blitz. Set aside until ready to use.

BUTTER CRAB FILLING Add the onion, garlic, and ginger to a hot saucepan with 1 Tbsp (15 mL) vegetable oil and sweat over medium heat for 1 minute. Add the cumin, turmeric, garam masala, cayenne, and salt and cook for another 30 seconds, stirring. Add the crushed tomatoes and cook for 2 minutes. Add the whipping cream and butter and stir together. Warm through for 5 minutes. Fold the peas, cumin potatoes, and crab meat into the filling, remove from heat, and allow to cool on a tray.

. . . recipe continued

SERVES 4

1 cup (375 mL) lump Dungeness crab meat

6 cups (1.5 L) vegetable oil

CUMIN POTATOES

2 cups (500 mL) peeled and finely diced russet potatoes

2 tsp (10 mL) vegetable oil

1 tsp (5 mL) cumin

Pinch of salt

PESHWARI DOUGH

2 cups (500 mL) all-purpose flour

¼ cup (60 mL) unsalted butter

2 Tbsp (30 mL) chopped raisins

2 Tbsp (30 mL) chopped dried apricots

¼ tsp (1 mL) salt

¼ tsp (1 mL) pepper

¼ tsp (1 mL) sugar

¼ cup (60 mL) water

CILANTRO CHUTNEY

2 cups (500 mL) cilantro

1 Tbsp (15 mL) chopped ginger

3 Tbsp (45 mL) lemon juice

¼ tsp (1 mL) salt

BUTTER CRAB FILLING

3 Tbsp (45 mL) diced onion

1 Tbsp (15 mL) diced garlic

2 Tbsp (30 mL) diced ginger

1 Tbsp (15 mL) vegetable oil

. . . ingredients continued

1 tsp (5 mL) cumin

¼ tsp (1 mL) turmeric

½ tsp (2.5 mL) garam masala

Pinch of cayenne

¼ tsp (1 mL) salt

2 Tbsp (30 mL) crushed tomatoes

⅓ cup (80 mL) whipping cream

2 Tbsp (30 mL) unsalted butter

⅓ cup (80 mL) frozen peas

TAMARIND DIP

2 Tbsp (30 mL) concentrated tamarind paste

3 Tbsp (45 mL) hot water

3 Tbsp (45 mL) brown sugar

½ tsp (2.5 mL) salt

1 tsp (5 mL) cumin

¼ tsp (1 mL) cayenne

GARNISH

Apricots

Raisins

Cilantro

TAMARIND DIP Add all the tamarind dip ingredients to a small pot and warm through for 10 minutes over low heat. Remove from heat and reserve.

SAMOSAS Heat 6 cups (1.5 L) vegetable oil in a heavy-bottomed pot until 350°F (175°C).

Remove the dough from the fridge. Cut it in half, then cut each half into 4 equal parts. Roll each piece into a ball between your hands. Using a rolling pin, roll each ball into a 4- to 6-inch (10 to 15 cm) circle, keeping a damp towel over the dough that is not being worked on.

Cut the first rolled-out circle in half, giving you 2 semicircles. Dip your finger in water and wet the edges of the semicircle, then bring the edges of the circle together to create a cone. Pinch the edges together along the outside of the cone, keeping the top open so that you can fill the samosa. Fill the cone with the butter crab filling and close it by pinching the edges together. Set onto a parchment-lined tray and cover with a damp towel until all the samosas have been prepared.

Lower 3 to 4 samosas into the frying oil and cook for 2 to 3 minutes until golden brown. Remove and place on a kitchen towel–lined tray. Repeat until all samosas are cooked.

Assembly

With a spoon, drizzle half of the tamarind dip around a plate and put the other half in a small ramekin for dipping. Scatter the butter crab samosas around the plate and add small pools of cilantro chutney for dipping, while also putting some in a ramekin. Scatter some raisins and apricots through the drizzle and decorate with a few cilantro leaves. Serve and enjoy!

FISH TIP

When I'm buying whole crab, I utilize it for a few different recipes. The legs and claws are great simply steamed and eaten with drawn butter, but the body meat and shells I use many other ways, including in these samosas. The shells are packed with flavour for the sauce, and the body meat works great for the filling.

P.S. The bigger the better when it comes to the crab.

CHAPTER NO. 5

NEW CLASSICS

Some of the best things in life are simple but effective. In this section,
I revisit some classic recipes, adding a Spencer Watts twist, and the outcome is
something new but familiar all at the same time.

CLASSIC INSPIRATION: MOULES MARINIÈRE
STEAMED P.E.I. MUSSELS 166
with French Fries / Whipped Mayonnaise / Gumbo Butter Broth

CLASSIC INSPIRATION: SCOTCH EGG
LOBSTER SCOTCH EGG 171
with Curry Mayo / Lobster Oil

CLASSIC INSPIRATION: GERMAN SCHNITZEL
PAN-FRIED CRISPY SOLE 174
with Grainy Mustard Spaetzle / Buttermilk–Dill Reduction

CLASSIC INSPIRATION: CLAMS AL VINO BLANCO
STEAMED LITTLE NECK CLAMS 179
with Sun-Dried Tomato and Basil Tapenade / Lemon Cream / Grilled Bread

CLASSIC INSPIRATION: FISH & CHIPS
CRISPY FISH AND CHIP SUSHI ROLL 182
with Tartar Sauce / Sesame Slaw / Potato Crumble

CLASSIC INSPIRATION: CASSOULET
SHELLFISH CASSOULET 187
with Lobster / Clams / Tarragon-Buttered Bread

CLASSIC INSPIRATION: SALT & PEPPER SQUID
SALT AND VINEGAR POTATO CHIP-CRUSTED CALAMARI 190
with Cucumber and Dill Dip

CLASSIC INSPIRATION: QUICHE LORRAINE
BAY SCALLOP AND SHRIMP QUICHE 195
with Caramelized Onions / Pancetta / Goat Cheese Royale / Spinach

CLASSIC INSPIRATION: SHRIMP SCAMPI
CREOLE SPICED PRAWNS 198
with Lemon Soy Butter

CLASSIC INSPIRATION: BACON-WRAPPED SCALLOPS
BLACK PEPPER SEA SCALLOPS 203
with Parsnip Purée / Pancetta and Medjool Date Marmalade

STEAMED P.E.I. MUSSELS

with French Fries / Whipped Mayonnaise / Gumbo Butter Broth

SERVES 2

1 lb (450 g) mussels, cleaned
and debearded

FRENCH FRIES

White flesh potatoes

8 cups (2 L) vegetable oil

Salt

WHIPPED MAYONNAISE

2 egg yolks

½ tsp (2.5 mL) Dijon mustard

2 tsp (10 mL) lemon juice

1 tsp (5 mL) salt

2 tsp (10 mL) red wine vinegar

1½ cups (375 mL) grapeseed oil

GUMBO BUTTER BROTH

1 Tbsp (15 mL) vegetable oil

⅓ cup (80 mL) diced onion

⅓ cup (80 mL) diced celery

⅓ cup (80 mL) diced green pepper

1 tsp (5 mL) diced garlic

5 oz (155 g) dried chorizo sausage
(1 link), sliced into coins

⅓ cup (80 mL) fish stock

2 Tbsp (30 mL) tomato purée

1 tsp (5 mL) smoked paprika

2 Tbsp (30 mL) white wine

1 tsp (5 mL) lemon juice

¼ tsp (1 mL) pepper

⅓ cup (80 mL) unsalted butter

⅓ cup (80 mL) chopped cilantro

GARNISH

Parsley, chopped

In one of the first professional kitchens I ever worked in, one of my many prep jobs was hand-whipping 2½ gallons (10 L) of mayo twice a week that was used for moules–frites (mussels and fries). This was in a restaurant at a French cultural centre where I was the only one who didn't speak any French. We had a "family meal" after most dinner services, and at one of these dinners I was given (by the owner, Chef Pascal) a bowl of mussels with hot, crispy handmade fries and a ramekin of my hand-whipped mayo. Along with that, I had a book of pictures from a famous French photographer, so I had something to look at while the rest of the team spoke French to each other. I didn't mind, as I loved being in my little corner of the restaurant at the end of service, eating my mussels and fries and dreaming about the future. This is my ode to that memory.

I serve these mussels in the pot I cooked them in and always remember to serve a discard bowl for the mussel shells.

"Sometimes you don't need a passport to travel."

Method

FRENCH FRIES Peel the potatoes and cut into evenly sized strips. Place in a large bowl and cover with water for 1 hour, changing the water when it becomes cloudy. Drain the water from the potatoes and pat dry.

Heat 8 cups (2 L) vegetable oil in a heavy-bottomed pot until it reaches 325°F (165°C). Place the fries into the oil and cook for 4 to 5 minutes; they will not be fully cooked. Remove the fries from the oil and place them on a paper-lined baking tray to reserve for additional frying.

Slowly bring the oil up to 375°F (190°C) while you prepare the mayonnaise and broth.

WHIPPED MAYONNAISE Add the egg yolks, Dijon mustard, lemon juice, salt, and red wine vinegar to a large mixing bowl. Add the oil in a slow and steady stream, whisking constantly, until the mayonnaise is thick and creamy.

. . . recipe continued

GUMBO BUTTER BROTH Heat 1 Tbsp (15 mL) vegetable oil in a large pot over medium-high heat. Add the onion, celery, green pepper, and garlic and sauté. Add the chorizo coins and sauté for another 30 seconds.

Add the fish stock, tomato purée, smoked paprika, white wine, lemon juice, pepper, and butter. Once the butter melts, add the mussels and cover with a lid. Cook for 3 to 4 minutes, until the mussels open.

FRENCH FRIES CONTINUED Carefully place the fries back into the hot oil and cook until golden and crispy. Season with salt.

Assembly

Once the mussels have finished cooking, discard any that do not open and add cilantro to the broth. Serve the mussels in the pot they were cooked in, and the fries piping hot with the whipped mayo in your favourite little bowl. Don't forget a discard bowl for the mussel shells!

FISH TIP

Mussels are a bang for your buck protein, but they still need a little care and attention. Always clean the outside of the mussels with a small knife or an abrasive scrubby.

To store them, make sure they are in the coldest part of the fridge, and place a dark towel over them. Never store them in water or "melting" ice. If you find any open mussels, make sure to discard them, but if they're closed, you're good to go.

LOBSTER SCOTCH EGG

with Curry Mayo / Lobster Oil

The very first time I had a Scotch egg . . . okay, wait, I'll paint you a picture. As the rain poured down on a cold November night in the big city, I was walking home and decided that I would stop for a drink, somewhere new, perhaps. I saw some people walk down some brick stairs and followed them into this tucked-away bar. It was dark, warm, and it smelled like memories. As the bartender poured my whisky, he said Scotch eggs were on the late night menu. And the rest was history. My version of this classic bar snack has luxurious lobster meat in place of the pork, with a super crunchy coating and side of whipped mayo. Paired with the essence of curry, this lobster Scotch egg is too much fun.

This classic bar snack can be dressed up or dressed down, so let your creative beast play and have some fun with it.

"Another whisky and Scotch egg? Absolutely, Eddie. Thank You."

Method

EGGS Bring a pot of water to a boil. Using a sharp needle or sharp wooden skewer, poke a hole in the bottom of each egg, just deep enough to pierce the shell, and place eggs in the boiling water. Cook for 6 minutes. Remove the eggs from the water and place immediately into a bowl full of water and ice. Allow to chill.

LOBSTER FARCE Pull the meat away from the lobster tails and set the shells in a bowl for later use.

Cut the uncooked lobster meat into chunks then add them, along with the salt, pepper, and tarragon, into a mini food processor. Blitz to create a coarse paste. Separate into 4 equal portions and reserve.

LOBSTER OIL Add the lobster shells reserved from the tails and all the lobster oil ingredients to a pot over medium heat; steep for 10 minutes. Strain into a clean bowl and reserve at room temperature.

CURRY MAYO Place all the curry mayo ingredient into a bowl and stir to combine. Set aside.

BREADING Break 3 eggs into a bowl and whisk to combine. In a separate bowl, add the panko, salt, and pepper; pour the flour into a third.

. . . recipe continued

SERVES 4

4 eggs

3 uncooked lobster tails
(I use frozen tails)

4 cups (1 L) vegetable oil

LOBSTER FARCE

¼ tsp (1 mL) salt

¼ tsp (1 mL) pepper

¼ tsp (1 mL) dried tarragon

LOBSTER OIL

1 cup (250 mL) grapeseed oil

1 clove garlic, crushed

¼ tsp (1 mL) salt

1 Tbsp (15 mL) smoked paprika

1 tsp (5 mL) sweet paprika

1 tsp (5 mL) chili flakes

CURRY MAYO

⅓ cup (80 mL) mayonnaise

2 Tbsp (30 mL) yogurt

1 tsp (5 mL) lemon juice

¼ tsp (1 mL) curry powder

¼ tsp (1 mL) turmeric

¼ tsp (1 mL) salt

½ tsp (2.5 mL) crushed garlic

. . . ingredients continued

BREADING

3 eggs

1½ cups (375 mL) panko
breadcrumbs

¼ tsp (1 mL) salt

¼ tsp (1 mL) pepper

1 cup (250 mL) all-purpose flour
+ more as needed

GARNISH

Baby greens

SCOTCH EGGS Heat 4 cups (1 L) vegetable oil in a heavy-bottomed pot until it reaches 375°F (190°C).

Peel the shells from the boiled eggs and roll the eggs in flour. Wet your hands and pack the portioned lobster farce around the eggs. Do not worry about the shape for now. Dip each farce-covered egg into the flour, then the beaten egg wash, then the panko mixture. Once covered in panko, reshape the eggs.

Gently lower the eggs into the oil and fry for 60 to 90 seconds. Remove the eggs from the oil and place on a paper-lined baking tray.

Assembly

Cut each Scotch egg in half and serve yolk side up on a bed of baby greens with a few dollops of curry mayo and a drizzle of lobster oil. Enjoy!

FISH TIP

When making lobster oil with lobster shells, I roast the shells first to bring out their aroma, then place them in cold neutral oil with the aromatics. I slowly bring the temperature up and steep to flavour the oil, ensuring not to boil as this would fry the aromatics and shells, leaving a burnt taste.

PAN-FRIED CRISPY SOLE

with Grainy Mustard Spaetzle / Buttermilk–Dill Reduction

4 sole fillets

Half a lemon, seared in a skillet or
on a grill until lightly charred,
for serving

GRAINY MUSTARD SPAETZLE

4 eggs

¾ cup (180 mL) milk

2 cups (500 mL) all-purpose flour

2 Tbsp (30 mL) grainy
Dijon mustard

Pinch of nutmeg

1 tsp (5 mL) salt + more as needed

Pinch of pepper + more as needed

1 Tbsp (15 mL) vegetable oil

BUTTERMILK–DILL REDUCTION

1 Tbsp (15 mL) vegetable oil

2 Tbsp (30 mL) diced shallots

1 tsp (5 mL) diced garlic

⅓ cup (80 mL) white wine

1 tsp (5 mL) white wine vinegar

1 cup (250 mL) whipping cream

⅓ cup (80 mL) buttermilk

¼ tsp (1 mL) dried dill

2 Tbsp (30 mL) capers

¼ tsp (1 mL) salt

¼ tsp (1 mL) pepper

. . . ingredients continued

I travelled to Germany with Culinary Team British Columbia to help compete in the IKA Culinary Olympics (the biggest culinary exhibition in the world). It also happened to be Oktoberfest while I was there. On an afternoon off, a teammate and I stumbled upon a massive Oktoberfest celebration in a town square in Erfurt. This is where I would have the best schnitzel of my life, along with many other European delicacies. I'll never forget the crunch, and the lemons served with it were paramount. My version has buttery sole and a fresh pasta called spaetzle, seasoned with mustard then fried until crisp. It's the perfect starch to drag through buttermilk sauce that's loaded with herbs, lemon, and garlic, which always reminds me of that magical day in Germany when we stumbled right into heaven.

A big plate is your best choice when serving this dish. You need enough room to soak up all that wonderful sauce and catch all that grilled lemon goodness.

"Are we in heaven? There's fried schnitzel and cold beer . . . we must be."

Method

GRAINY MUSTARD SPAETZLE Combine the eggs and half of the milk in a bowl with the flour, Dijon mustard, nutmeg, salt, and pepper. Whisk in the remaining milk, 1 Tbsp (15 mL) at a time, until you have a batter that has some thickness, but is still thin enough to pass through your colander easily. Allow the batter to rest for 15 minutes.

Place a pot of salted water on the stove and bring to a boil. Push all the spaetzle batter through the perforated holes in the colander, over the water, creating droplets of batter that fall into the water. Cook the dough until it floats, then remove and place on a parchment-lined baking tray with a splash of oil.

BUTTERMILK–DILL REDUCTION Heat 1 Tbsp (15 mL) vegetable oil in a pan over medium-high heat. Add the shallots and sweat for 30 seconds. Add the garlic and cook another half-minute. Add the white wine and white wine vinegar, simmer, and reduce until the pan is almost dry. Add the whipping cream, buttermilk, dill, and capers, and season with salt and pepper. Reduce until the sauce is thick enough to coat the back of a spoon. Keep warm for plating.

. . . recipe continued

SOLE DREDGE Heat ½ cup (125 mL) vegetable oil in a frying pan until it reaches 350 to 375°F (175 to 190°C).

Set up the dredging station with the flour on a plate, the beaten egg in a bowl, and the panko with parsley, salt, and pepper mixed together in a third bowl. Dredge each piece of sole in flour, then egg, then panko.

Place the fish in the oil and cook 1 minute per side.

SPAETZLE CONTINUED Heat 1 Tbsp (15 mL) vegetable oil in a frying pan over medium-high heat. Add the cooked spaetzle, season with salt and pepper, and fry until golden.

SOLE DREDGE

½ cup (125 mL) vegetable oil

1 cup (250 mL) all-purpose flour

2 eggs, beaten

1 cup (250 mL) panko breadcrumbs

2 tsp (10 mL) chopped parsley

¼ tsp (1 mL) salt

¼ tsp (1 mL) pepper

Assembly

Place the grainy mustard spaetzle on a plate with the sole and a drizzle of warm buttermilk–dill reduction. Serve with grilled lemons.

FISH TIP

My preferred method of skinning fresh sole is simple. Make a small incision across the tail where the tail meets the flesh. With a dry kitchen towel, slowly grab the skin and peel it back. This will remove the skin and keep the flesh intact. You can do this to both sides.

STEAMED LITTLE NECK CLAMS

with Sun-Dried Tomato and Basil Tapenade /
Lemon Cream / Grilled Bread

My mom loves buttery clams swimming in a divine sauce of wine, garlic, and butter. This addiction started with her visits to a Spanish tapas bar where I was working when I was a young cook. Since then, whenever I get the chance I go to our local fish market to buy a few pounds of fresh clams and a loaf of crispy bread for us to enjoy. This is the only time in our life when the room is quiet.

I serve these clams up in a big bowl with lots of room for sauce. Remember, you will need a vessel to discard the shells into, along with spoons and a small bakery's worth of bread.

"I don't know what you're doing, but it's the same thing I'm trying to do: no talking."

Method

SUN-DRIED TOMATO AND BASIL TAPENADE Place the basil, sun-dried tomatoes, garlic, salt, pepper, and olive oil into a mini food processor. Blitz into a pesto. Reserve until ready to serve.

LEMON CREAM Heat 1 Tbsp (15 mL) vegetable oil in a heavy-bottomed pot over medium-high heat. Add the shallot and garlic and sweat. Add the white wine and deglaze the pan; reduce for 60 to 90 seconds. Add the lemon juice, whipping cream, salt, pepper, and chili flakes and slowly reduce the mixture until the sauce coats the back of a spoon.

GRILLED BREAD Preheat a cast iron grill pan over high heat.

Mix the garlic, parsley, salt, and melted butter in a bowl. Cut the baguette lengthwise in 1-inch (2.5 cm) slices and paint both sides of the bread with the butter mixture. Place the bread on the grill pan, cut side down, for 1 to 2 minutes, until char marks appear.

CLAMS Add the little neck clams to the thickened lemon cream and cover with a lid. Steam for 1 to 2 minutes and finish with chopped parsley, fresh lemon juice, and chili flakes.

. . . *recipe continued*

SERVES 2 TO 4

2 lb (900 g) fresh little neck clams

SUN-DRIED TOMATO AND BASIL TAPENADE

½ cup (125 mL) basil

½ cup (125 mL) sun-dried tomatoes

1 tsp (5 mL) chopped garlic

¼ tsp (1 mL) salt

¼ tsp (1 mL) pepper

2 Tbsp (30 mL) olive oil

LEMON CREAM

1 Tbsp (15 mL) vegetable oil

1 medium shallot, diced

1 Tbsp (15 mL) minced garlic

½ cup (125 mL) white wine

1 Tbsp (15 mL) lemon juice

1 cup (250 mL) whipping cream

¼ tsp (1 mL) salt

¼ tsp (1 mL) pepper

¼ tsp (1 mL) chili flakes

GRILLED BREAD

1 tsp (5 mL) minced garlic

1 Tbsp (15 mL) chopped parsley

¼ tsp (1 mL) salt

¼ cup (60 mL) melted unsalted butter

Half a baguette

GARNISH

1 Tbsp (15 mL) chopped parsley

1 tsp (5 mL) lemon juice

Chili flakes

Assembly

Spread some of the tapenade over the grilled bread. Place the little neck clams in a big bowl and serve immediately—piping hot! Don't forget the discard bowl for the clam shells.

FISH TIP

Fresh clams are not like mussels. Mussels need to be cleaned before the cooking process; clams, on the other hand, are ready to go. I always make sure my clams smell fresh. If any clams are slightly open, tap the open part of the shell. If it closes, they are fresh; if not, then discard. If you're storing the clams, make sure to keep them cold and in the dark.

CRISPY FISH AND CHIP SUSHI ROLL

with Tartar Sauce / Sesame Slaw / Potato Crumble

8 oz (230 g) cod, cut into
thin strips

6 cups (1.5 L) vegetable oil

Salt, to taste

Pepper, to taste

4 nori sheets

Sweet soy sauce, for serving

TARTAR SAUCE

⅓ cup (80 mL) mayonnaise

1 Tbsp (15 mL) minced shallots

2 Tbsp (30 mL) minced dill pickles

1 Tbsp (15 mL) finely
chopped capers

½ tsp (2.5 mL) minced garlic

½ tsp (2.5 mL) lemon juice

¼ tsp (1 mL) salt

¼ tsp (1 mL) dried dill

¼ tsp (1 mL) pepper

SESAME SLAW

2 Tbsp (30 mL) mayonnaise

2 tsp (10 mL) sesame seeds

¼ tsp (1 mL) sesame oil

¼ tsp (1 mL) sugar

¼ tsp (1 mL) rice wine vinegar

¼ tsp (1 mL) salt

¼ tsp (1 mL) pepper

1 cup (250 mL) shredded
green cabbage

1 cup (250 mL) shredded
red cabbage

. . . ingredients continued

I love a good classic plate of fish and chips—I mean, what's not to like? Sweet fish wrapped in a light and crunchy beer batter, served with crispy fries and a sharp tartar sauce. This new twist on an old classic respects everything you love about the classic, but serves it up with a modern look, and adds some sticky rice to bring it all together.

These are so beautiful on their own, they don't need a lot of fancy plating. Serve on a simple flat white plate with drizzles of sauce for dipping, and watch them disappear.

"The Fish and Chip Roll—the definition of a new classic."

Method

TARTAR SAUCE Place all the tartar sauce ingredients into a bowl and combine well. Cover and refrigerate until ready to use.

SESAME SLAW Combine the mayonnaise, sesame seeds, sesame oil, sugar, vinegar, salt, and pepper in a large bowl. Fold in the shredded cabbages until coated with the dressing. Cover and store in the fridge.

STICKY RICE Rinse the rice under cold water until the water runs clear. Cook according to the package instructions. Once cooked, allow the rice to rest with the lid on for 10 minutes.

While the rice cooks, add the rice wine vinegar, sugar, and salt to a small saucepan and heat over low. Cook until the sugar and salt have dissolved, then reduce to ¼ cup (60 mL).

Place the cooked rice into a non-reactive (glass, wood) bowl and drizzle with the rice wine vinegar sauce. Cover the rice with a damp kitchen towel and set aside.

BEER BATTER Whisk the flour, baking powder, salt, and turmeric together in a bowl. Slowly whisk in the beer until the batter is no longer lumpy.

COD Add 6 cups (1.5 L) vegetable oil to a heavy-bottomed pot and heat over medium-high until it reaches 375°F (190°C). Season the cod with salt and pepper and dust with flour.

. . . recipe continued

STICKY RICE

3 cups (750 mL) uncooked
sushi rice

⅔ cup (160 mL) rice wine vinegar

3 Tbsp (45 mL) sugar

1½ Tbsp (22 mL) salt

BEER BATTER

1 cup (250 mL) all-purpose flour
+ extra for dusting fish

1 tsp (5 mL) baking powder

¼ tsp (1 mL) salt

⅛ tsp (0.5 mL) turmeric

1½ cups (375 mL) cold beer

POTATO CRUMBLE

1 cup (250 mL) peeled and diced
russet potato

1½ cups (375 mL) water

1 cup (250 mL) vegetable oil

GARNISH

Pea shoots

Pickled ginger

Wasabi

SPECIAL EQUIPMENT

Bamboo rolling mat

Dip the cod into the beer batter and ensure it is fully coated. Slowly lower it into the oil. Fry the fish for 3 to 4 minutes until golden brown. Remove and place on a kitchen towel–lined tray. Retain the hot oil for the potato crumble.

POTATO CRUMBLE Place the peeled and diced russet potato into a blender with the 1½ cups (375 mL) water. Blitz for 30 to 45 seconds then strain through a fine mesh sieve. (The size should be comparable to rock salt.) Drain and rinse the potatoes. Place the pulverized potatoes into a bowl lined with a kitchen towel and pat dry.

Using the same oil as the fish, fry the potato crumble until golden. Drain onto a paper-lined tray and season with salt.

Assembly

Wrap a bamboo sushi mat in plastic wrap. Lay a sheet of nori on the mat, shiny side down. Dampen your fingers and place a lemon-size ball of rice in the centre of the nori sheet. Using your fingers, spread the rice across the entire sheet of nori. Press the rice down firmly. You should not be able to see the nori through the rice, but if you use too much, it will not roll properly.

Flip the rice-covered nori so that the rice is now on the bottom. Cover a 2-inch (5 cm) section of nori with sesame slaw and place a piece of cooked cod on the slaw. Using the mat and rolling away from you, tightly roll the nori around the fish. Overlap slightly at the end of the roll and press lightly to seal. Repeat with each piece of fish.

Using a sharp knife, gently cut the roll in half, then cut each half into 4 bite-size pieces. Stagger the cut rolls in a line, drizzle with sweet soy sauce, and place a dollop of tartar sauce on each piece. Sprinkle the potato crumble and pea shoots overtop. Serve with soy sauce, pickled ginger, and wasabi. Enjoy!

FISH TIP

An easy way to know when your oil is hot enough to deep-fry is to drop a single popcorn kernel into the oil while it heats. It will pop when the oil is between 360 and 375°F (180 to 190°C). Remove the kernel and you are ready to deep-fry!

SHELLFISH CASSOULET

with Lobster / Clams / Tarragon-Buttered Bread

The first time I had a classic cassoulet, I was immediately in love with the richness and the amount of flavour packed into this little dish. My version packs the same punch but is chock full of seafood. The richness from the sausage and lobster stock gives a twist to an old classic that sticks to your ribs.

Cassoulet gets its name from the dish it's cooked and served in. I place mine on a trivet with a big serving spoon and we all dig in.

"In the unlikely event of an emergency, your chair can also be used as a bed."

Method

LOBSTER STOCK Heat 1 Tbsp (15 mL) olive oil in a large saucepan over medium-high heat. Add the onion, garlic, carrots, and celery and sauté for 2 to 3 minutes until the onion is translucent. Add the lobster head and shells (reserve the meat for later) and cook for another 2 to 3 minutes. Use the back of a wooden spoon to crush the shells as you sauté. Add the rest of the lobster stock ingredients and slowly reduce the stock from 6 cups (1.5 L) to 2 cups (500 mL). Reserve.

TARRAGON BUTTER Combine all the tarragon butter ingredients in a small bowl and whip until smooth and creamy.

Cut 6 incisions through the demi baguette, like an accordion. Do not cut through the bottom of the bread. With a spatula, spread the tarragon butter in between each crevice and bake for 3 minutes just before serving.

SHELLFISH CASSOULET Preheat oven to 375°F (190°C).

Heat 1 tsp (5 mL) vegetable oil in a heavy-bottomed pot over medium-high heat. Add the halved sausage links and sear; remove and set aside until later. Add the onion, garlic, carrots, and celery and sweat in the fat left behind by the sausages. Add the butter and flour to the vegetables and stir to create a roux.

. . . recipe continued

SERVES 4 TO 6

1 whole precooked lobster

10 medium-size clams, fresh

Demi baguette, for serving

LOBSTER STOCK

1 Tbsp (15 mL) olive oil

1 medium onion, chopped

3 cloves garlic, chopped

1 cup (250 mL) chopped carrots

1 cup (250 mL) chopped celery

1 bay leaf

2 sprigs thyme

1 tsp (5 mL) paprika

1 tsp (5 mL) seafood seasoning

6 cups (1.5 L) beef broth

TARRAGON BUTTER

¾ cup (180 mL) unsalted butter

½ tsp (2.5 mL) dried tarragon

½ tsp (2.5 mL) minced garlic

1 tsp (5 mL) lemon zest

¼ tsp (1 mL) salt

¼ tsp (1 mL) pepper

Pinch of chili flakes

. . . ingredients continued

SHELLFISH CASSOULET

1 tsp (5 mL) vegetable oil

5 raw chorizo sausage links, halved

½ cup (125 mL) diced onion

1 Tbsp (15 mL) crushed garlic

½ cup (125 mL) diced carrots

½ cup (125 mL) diced celery

2 Tbsp (30 mL) unsalted butter

2½ Tbsp (40 mL) all-purpose flour

Salt, to taste

Pepper, to taste

2 cups (500 mL) canned cannellini beans, drained

2½ Tbsp (40 mL) tomato purée

¼ cup (60 mL) chopped parsley

Continue to stir until you achieve a paste-like consistency; while stirring, add the lobster stock ½ cup (125 mL) at a time, making sure the mixture thickens before each further addition. Season with salt and pepper. Add the cannellini beans and tomato purée and cook for 1 minute more. Chop the lobster meat and add it, along with the raw clams and parsley, then add the sausage back into the cassoulet. Transfer to an ovenproof casserole dish and bake in the oven for 10 minutes. Place the bread in the oven for the last 3 minutes. Remove the cassoulet and bread and serve.

FISH TIP

When making lobster stock with the shells and bodies, I always remove the gills from the lobster, which have a tendency to leave behind a bitter taste. Gills are super easy to remove—just pinch with your fingers and gently pull away from the body. This can be done once the rest of the lobster has been cleaned.

SALT AND VINEGAR POTATO CHIP-CRUSTED CALAMARI

with Cucumber and Dill Dip

SERVES 4 TO 6

8 oz (230 g) squid rings

CUCUMBER AND DILL DIP

⅓ cup (80 mL) sour cream

⅓ cup (80 mL) mayonnaise

¼ cup (60 mL) diced, peeled, and seeded cucumber

½ tsp (2.5 mL) grated garlic

¼ tsp (1 mL) dried dill

½ Tbsp (7.5 mL) lemon juice

¼ tsp (1 mL) salt

¼ tsp (1 mL) pepper

CALAMARI DREDGE

6 cups (1.5 L) vegetable oil

1½ cups (375 mL) salt and vinegar potato chip crumbs (about half a large bag)

1½ cups (375 mL) Italian breadcrumbs

5 eggs, beaten

1 cup (250 mL) all-purpose flour

Salt, to taste

GARNISH

Lemon wedges

Cucumber, sliced

Eating calamari at a pub or restaurant is the perfect snack. Just think of it . . . you can eat it with your fingers, it's a super crispy and a great vessel for delicious dips, plus it only takes minutes to prepare. My version has a crazy salt and vinegar potato chip crust that will have you dipping and licking your fingers.

Use a long plate that reaches down the table so everyone can get their hands in. Serve it with lemons and seafood forks, and dive in!

"Ever had something so delicious and crispy you contemplated studying black magic, sorcery, and the dark arts to discover the unknown secrets of crunch?"

Method

CUCUMBER AND DILL DIP Combine all the cucumber and dill dip ingredients in a bowl and mix well. Cover and refrigerate until ready to serve.

CALAMARI DREDGE Heat 6 cups (1.5 L) vegetable oil in a heavy-bottomed pot until it reaches 360 to 375°F (185 to 190°C).

Add the salt and vinegar potato chips to a food processor and blitz to a crumb. Move the crumbs to a large bowl and mix with the Italian breadcrumbs. Crack eggs into a separate bowl and whisk. Pour the flour into a third bowl.

Rinse the squid rings and pat dry. Toss in the flour and shake off the excess (I use a strainer to make this easy and mess free). Dip the calamari in the egg wash and shake off the excess. (This is a great place for a second strainer if you have one. Tongs work, too.) Coat the calamari in the salt and vinegar crumb mix.

Place half of the coated calamari into the oil and fry for 30 to 60 seconds until golden brown. Remove and place on a paper-lined baking tray and season with salt. Repeat with the remaining coated calamari.

Assembly

Pile the calamari on a long plate with the cucumber and dill dip in the middle. Add lemon wedges and cucumber slices and serve warm. Enjoy!

. . recipe continued

. . . Salt and Vinegar Potato Chip–Crusted Calamari (continued)

FISH TIP

Calamari is super fun to make at home. The rule with squid is, depending on what you plan to do with it, you either cook it in seconds or hours. This particular recipe is flash-fried in just 45 seconds.

Make sure your sauces are ready, and the last step before eating is frying the squid. Serve it right away and don't forget the lemons! Most importantly, make sure you're always having fun.

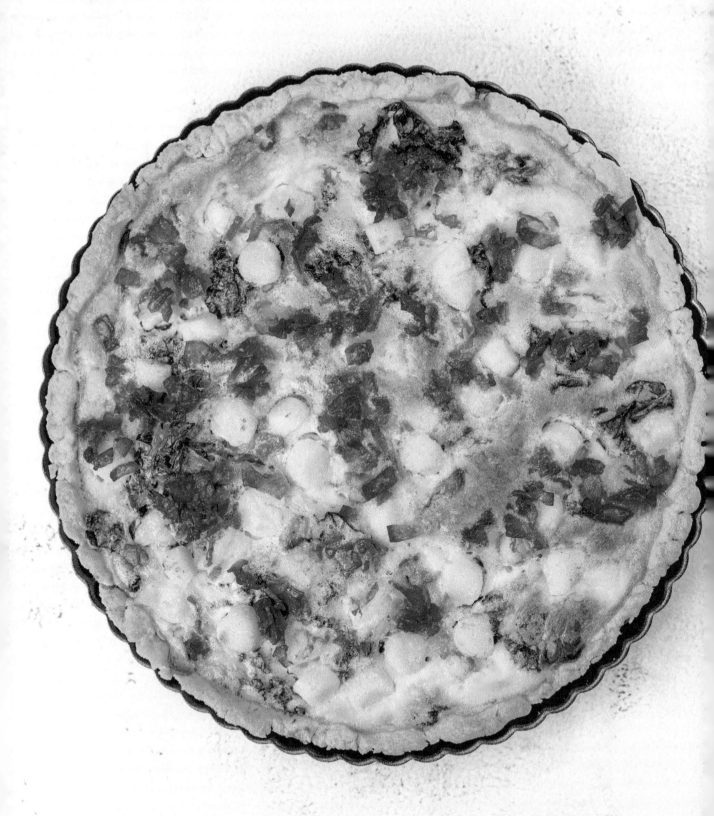

BAY SCALLOP AND SHRIMP QUICHE

with Caramelized Onions / Pancetta / Goat Cheese Royale / Spinach

Between the perfect pastry crust and the creamy filling of egg with goat cheese, shrimp, scallops, caramelized onion, and pancetta, this might be the perfect bite of food. A quiche is something that looks simple, but has some serious technique involved in the preparation. I mastered the art of quiche while working in a French bistro, and trust me when I tell you, making three a day will make anyone an expert. The ratio between egg, cream, and goat cheese makes the perfect texture inside. I happily share that with you, my friends.

I serve this quiche on a cake tower with a cake spatula. It's the savoury version of a cake, so why not? Plus it looks super cool.

"First time I had quiche, it was so good I forgot where I was for about 10 minutes."

Method

QUICHE CRUST Add 1 cup (250 mL) butter and the flour to a food processor and pulse until you reach a crumbly sand-like consistency. Add the ice water slowly until a dough is formed. Remove the dough and knead gently until smooth. Wrap the dough in plastic and place in the fridge to rest for 30 minutes.

Preheat oven to 375°F (190°C).

Lightly dust your counter with flour and roll out the pie dough into a circle about 2 inches (5 cm) bigger than your pie dish. Press the dough into the pie plate. Cover with parchment paper and place uncooked dried beans on top to act as weights. Blind bake the pie crust for 25 minutes.

While the pie shell is blind baking, prepare the fillings.

CARAMELIZED ONIONS Heat 1 Tbsp (15 mL) vegetable oil in a frying pan over medium-high heat. Add the onions, thyme, salt, and pepper. Sauté until the onions are golden brown. Reserve until ready to assemble the quiche.

PANCETTA Heat 1 Tbsp (15 mL) vegetable oil in a frying pan over medium heat. Add the diced pancetta and cook until crispy. Drain on a kitchen towel and reserve until ready to build.

. . . *recipe continued*

SERVES 6 TO 8

5 oz (155 g) bay scallops, chopped

5 oz (155 g) shrimp, peeled and deveined (see Fish Tip, page 201), chopped

QUICHE CRUST

1 cup (250 mL) unsalted butter

2 cups (500 mL) all-purpose flour + more for dusting

2 to 3 Tbsp (30 to 45 mL) ice water

CARAMELIZED ONIONS

1 Tbsp (15 mL) vegetable oil

2 medium Spanish onions, thinly sliced

¼ tsp (1 mL) chopped fresh thyme

¼ tsp (1 mL) salt

¼ tsp (1 mL) pepper

PANCETTA

1 Tbsp (15 mL) vegetable oil

⅓ cup (80 mL) diced pancetta

GOAT CHEESE ROYALE

¼ cup (60 mL) goat cheese

2 cups (500 mL) whipping cream

4 eggs

¼ tsp (1 mL) salt

¼ tsp (1 mL) pepper

SPINACH

1 Tbsp (15 mL) vegetable oil

1 Tbsp (15 mL) unsalted butter

2 cups (500 mL) chopped spinach

¼ tsp (1 mL) salt

¼ tsp (1 mL) pepper

GOAT CHEESE ROYALE Add all the goat cheese royale ingredients into a blender and blend until smooth. Reserve.

SPINACH Heat 1 Tbsp (15 mL) vegetable oil and 1 Tbsp (15 mL) butter in a frying pan over medium-high heat. Once the butter has melted, add the spinach and season with salt and pepper. Cook while flipping and turning the spinach until wilted. Remove from heat.

QUICHE Take the pie shell out of the oven and remove the parchment and beans. (Leave the oven at 375°F/190°C for the quiche.) Add the caramelized onions to the pie shell. Add the spinach and sprinkle scallops, shrimp, and pancetta evenly over the onion. Pour the goat cheese royale overtop and place the quiche in the oven. Bake for 25 minutes until golden brown and the royale is firm.

FISH TIP

Small bay scallops usually have a muscle on the side. This needs to be removed before cooking, as it's super chewy and a no-go, so make sure to remove and discard. What you're left with is a perfectly plump little scallop.

CREOLE SPICED PRAWNS

with Lemon Soy Butter

SERVES 2 TO 4

12 oz (340 g) jumbo prawns, shell on

1 Tbsp (15 mL) vegetable oil

CREOLE SPICE MIXTURE

¼ tsp (1 mL) cayenne

1 Tbsp (15 mL) smoked paprika

1 Tbsp (15 mL) lemon zest

1 tsp (5 mL) diced garlic

1 tsp (5 mL) dried oregano

¼ tsp (1 mL) salt

¼ tsp (1 mL) pepper

2 Tbsp (30 mL) chopped cilantro

2 Tbsp (30 mL) olive oil

LEMON SOY BUTTER

½ tsp (2.5 mL) lemon juice

½ tsp (2.5 mL) soy sauce

½ cup (125 mL) unsalted butter, cold, cubed

GARNISH

Cilantro, chopped

What do you make for a female rock and roll legend? Well . . . Creole spiced prawns and way too much butter sauce. This happened to me when I was invited over to a musical icon's house to have dinner. I brought fresh prawns, unsalted butter, lemons, and an arsenal of spices. With John Coltrane playing so loud the gin vibrated in my cocktail, and butter dripping down to our elbows, we peeled and ate prawns like savages. This would happen more than once in my life and those memories will be kept in the "I can't believe that happened to me category."

"They paved paradise and put up a prawn shop."

Method

CREOLE SPICE MIXTURE Add the cayenne, smoked paprika, lemon zest, garlic, oregano, salt, pepper, cilantro, and olive oil to a small bowl and whisk. With a clean pair of kitchen scissors, cut the shell along the top of each prawns (the thick part) until you reach the bottom of the tail. Add the prawns to the spice mixture and toss to coat. Reserve.

LEMON SOY BUTTER Combine the lemon juice and soy sauce in a saucepan over medium-low heat. Add one cube of butter at a time and allow it to melt while you swirl the pan constantly. As each cube of butter emulsifies, add another. Keep the pan moving until all the butter has melted. Keep warm while preparing the prawns.

PRAWNS Add 1 Tbsp (15 mL) olive oil and the Creole spiced prawns to a hot skillet. Cook for 1 minute on each side.

Assembly

Line the prawns up on a plate in a straight line, drizzle with the lemon soy butter, and garnish with cilantro. Enjoy!

. . . recipe continued

FISH TIP

This recipe calls for shrimp with their shells on. When working with shell-on shrimp, you may need to devein them. This sounds intimidating but don't worry, it's very simple. I cut the shells along the back with a good pair of kitchen scissors and use my knife to make a small cut along the length of the tail. This exposes the shrimp, and you will see a dark vein. Remove it with the tip of a small knife and give the shrimp a quick rinse under cold water. Your shrimp are now ready for the flavour spa.

BLACK PEPPER SEA SCALLOPS

with Parsnip Purée / Pancetta and Medjool Date Marmalade

Bacon-wrapped scallops remind me of going to our local steakhouse when we were kids. It was such a treat. So was watching my dad get yelled at by our server for sticking his finger in the blue cheese dressing at the salad bar. Gotta love the 80s! That was the inspiration for this dish, minus the yelling and blue cheese.

Get your nice plates out! This dish looks so great when individually plated. I use a white flat plate to contrast the bacon and dates. Don't be afraid to use one of your bigger plates—negative space is your friend.

"hey dad! look out! he's coming for ya."

Method

PARSNIP PURÉE Pour 1½ cups (375 mL) water into a pot and bring to a boil. Add the parsnips, butter, shallots, and salt, and cook until soft. Put the parsnips into a blender and purée to a soft and smooth consistency. If the purée is too thick, add 1 Tbsp (15 mL) water until you reach the desired consistency. Return the purée to a pot and keep warm.

PANCETTA AND MEDJOOL DATE MARMALADE Add 1 Tbsp (15 mL) olive oil and the diced pancetta to a skillet on medium to high heat. Cook until the pancetta starts to crisp, then add the shallots and cook for another 30 seconds. Add the rest of the marmalade ingredients and lower the temperature. Reduce to a thick, jammy texture and reserve.

SCALLOPS Remove the muscle from each scallop. Pat the scallops dry and season with salt and pepper. Heat 1 Tbsp (15 mL) olive oil in a frying pan over high heat and sear the scallops on both sides for 1 minute per side.

Assembly

To plate, begin with the parsnip purée on the plate. Place the scallops on the purée and top with the marmalade. Enjoy!

... recipe continued

SERVES 4

12 large sea scallops

1 Tbsp (15 mL) olive oil

¼ tsp (1 mL) salt

¼ tsp (1 mL) cracked black pepper

PARSNIP PURÉE

½ cup (125 mL) chopped parsnips

2 Tbsp (30 mL) unsalted butter

¼ cup (60 mL) diced shallots

½ tsp (2.5 mL) salt

PANCETTA AND MEDJOOL DATE MARMALADE

1 Tbsp (15 mL) olive oil

½ cup (125 mL) diced pancetta

¼ cup (60 mL) diced shallots

½ cup (125 mL) diced Medjool dates

¼ tsp (1 mL) salt

½ tsp (2.5 mL) red wine vinegar

1 tsp (5 mL) brown sugar

FISH TIP

When cooking scallops, remember that they cook very fast. For me, the perfect scallop is cooked medium. Once cooked, the scallop should still have some bounce to it.

Whenever I make scallops, it's always the last task to be done. Everything else is ready to go, and I cook them start to finish in a pan on the stovetop.

BONUS TIP: I only flip them once.

FAMILY STYLE

This section is filled to the brim with exciting seafood dishes that pack flavour and feed the whole gang. Whether it's Sunday dinner or an easy weekday meal, this section will inspire anyone who's trying to feed the fam!

PANKO HERB-CRUSTED SIDE OF SALMON 208
with Bacon Potato Salad

MISO HONEY-GLAZED SALMON RICE BOWLS 213
with Brown Butter Mushrooms / Bok Choy

FISHERMAN'S PIE 216
with Puff Pastry "Barnacles"

SAN FRANCISCO CIOPPINO 221
with Mussels / Clams / Jumbo Shrimp / Sole

SEAFOOD-STUFFED JUMBO SHELLS 224
with Puttanesca Sauce / Braised Spinach /
Crab and Ricotta Stuffing / Garlic Shrimp

BBQ GLAZED BLACK COD PIZZA 229
with Hoison Pizza Sauce / Chili Ginger Marmalade / Asian Greens

PIRI PIRI-MARINATED COD FILLETS 232
with Salsa Verde / Orzo Succotash

SMOKY TOMATO RISOTTO 237
with Ling Cod / Mussels / Clams / Shrimp

HAWAIIAN FAMILY DINNER 240
with Halibut Steaks / BBQ Pork Rice / Tropical Salsa

ALMOND-CRUSTED TROUT 245
with Gruyère Galette / Grape Beurre Blanc

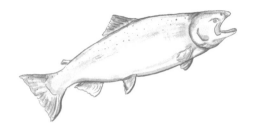

PANKO HERB-CRUSTED SIDE OF SALMON

with Bacon Potato Salad

SERVES 4 TO 6

2 lb (900 g) side of Atlantic salmon

Lemon wedges, for serving

BACON POTATO SALAD

24 baby potatoes, peeled and quartered

1 Tbsp (15 mL) vegetable oil

8 slices bacon, diced

2 Tbsp (30 mL) diced shallots

1 Tbsp (15 mL) crushed garlic

2 Tbsp (30 mL) chopped fresh parsley

2 Tbsp (30 mL) sherry vinegar

2 Tbsp (30 mL) olive oil

¼ tsp (1 mL) salt

¼ tsp (1 mL) pepper

SALMON

3 Tbsp (45 mL) mayonnaise

2 Tbsp (30 mL) panko breadcrumbs

½ cup (125 mL) fresh parsley

1 tsp (5 mL) crushed garlic

3 Tbsp (45 mL) lemon zest

¼ tsp (1 mL) salt

¼ tsp (1 mL) pepper

This recipe is so simple, but it's in this book because it's a staple in our home and everyone loves it, kids included. The herbs and panko give the delicate salmon great flavour and crunch, and you will never look at potato salad the same way again.

I bake this salmon on a foil-lined baking sheet and that is exactly how I serve it. Engage "wow" factor.

"When my children leave the 'nest,' they will know how to make this blindfolded."

Method

BACON POTATO SALAD Boil the potatoes in a pot of water over high heat until fork tender. Drain the water and pat the potatoes dry; slightly crush or flatten the potatoes with the back of a spoon then place them into a bowl.

Heat 1 Tbsp (15 mL) vegetable oil in a skillet over medium-high heat. Add the bacon and cook until crispy. Reserve the cooked bacon and add the fat from the pan to a small bowl. Add the shallots, garlic, parsley, sherry vinegar, olive oil, salt, and pepper to the bowl and whisk to combine, then pour over the potatoes. Add the bacon and toss to coat. Cover with plastic wrap and reserve.

SALMON Preheat oven to 400°F (200°C).

Leaving the skin on the salmon, place the side of salmon onto a foil-lined baking tray and crinkle the foil around the fish to capture any juices that may leak out while cooking. Pat the salmon dry with a kitchen towel. Brush the entire side of salmon with the mayonnaise.

In a miniature food processor, blitz the panko, parsley, garlic, lemon zest, salt, and pepper. Pack the breadcrumb mixture over the surface of the salmon and press into the mayonnaise to create a crust.

Bake the salmon in the oven for 20 minutes. The internal temperature should be 150°F (65°C) when cooked perfectly medium and tender in the middle.

. . . recipe continued

Assembly

Serve the salmon on the foil and the potato salad in a nice family style bowl. Add the lemon wedges and enjoy!

FISH TIP

When cooking fish, science and temperature are your friends. Having a good thermometer by your side is a wonderful tool. For salmon, there is no resting involved, so when the temperature hits 150°F (65°C), this is when I pull it from the oven. This will give you salmon that is cooked medium. For me, this is the perfect temperature for salmon.

MISO HONEY-GLAZED SALMON RICE BOWLS

with Brown Butter Mushrooms / Bok Choy

Rice bowls are a carnival of flavour, colour, and texture. This bowl has it all from glazed salmon to the perfect fluffy rice, topped with brown butter and lemon-scented mushrooms. Don't be surprised if this salmon bowl shows up on the dinner table on the regular. It's hearty, and this recipe makes it easy to feed a lot of hungry mouths.

It says it all in the name. I serve these in wide, deep bowls with chopsticks and a big spoon. They look amazing and it's all about that flavour, baby!

"Imagine you're playing the claw arcade game and the claw comes up holding $1500 cash."

Method

MISO HONEY GLAZE Combine the miso, honey, soy sauce, sesame oil, sesame seeds, lemon juice, and egg yolk in a bowl; gradually whisk in the olive oil. Continue whisking until the glaze is thick.

Place the salmon in a glass dish and cover with the glaze. Cover with plastic wrap and place in the fridge to marinate for 1 to 2 hours, or overnight at the longest.

RICE Cook the rice according to the package instructions and set aside.

SALMON Preheat oven to 475°F (245°C).

Remove the fish from the marinade and place it on a baking sheet covered with non-stick foil, keeping as much of the sticky marinade on the fish as possible. Note that the oven is very hot, so I do not recommend using parchment, which could catch fire.

Place the baking sheet on the top rack of the oven and cook for 8 minutes, or until the fish is crispy on top. The internal temperature of the salmon should be 150°F (65°C) when cooked medium, tender, and juicy in the middle.

While the fish cooks, prepare the mushrooms and bok choy.

BROWN BUTTER MUSHROOMS Place a small saucepan over high heat (you want the pan really hot). Add the butter—this is going to smoke, which is a good thing. Let the butter cook until it starts to turn a deep amber colour and smells nutty. Turn off the heat and add the soy sauce and lemon juice. Reserve.

. . . recipe continued

SERVES 4

Four 6 oz (170 g) salmon fillets

MISO HONEY GLAZE

1 Tbsp (15 mL) white miso

3 Tbsp (45 mL) honey

½ Tbsp (7.5 mL) soy sauce

1 tsp (5 mL) sesame oil

1 Tbsp (15 mL) sesame seeds

1 tsp (5 mL) lemon juice

1 egg yolk

½ cup (125 mL) olive oil

RICE

2 cups (500 mL) uncooked short grain rice

BROWN BUTTER MUSHROOMS

⅓ cup (80 mL) unsalted butter

½ Tbsp (7.5 mL) soy sauce

1 tsp (5 mL) lemon juice

1 Tbsp (15 mL) olive oil

3 cups (750 mL) chopped mixed mushrooms

2 Tbsp (30 mL) shallots

BOK CHOY

½ tsp (2.5 mL) vegetable oil

½ tsp (2.5 mL) sesame oil

4 baby bok choy, halved lengthwise

1 tsp (5 mL) diced garlic

1 Tbsp (15 mL) diced ginger

½ tsp (2.5 mL) salt

¼ cup (60 mL) water

GARNISH

Sesame seeds

Heat 1 Tbsp (15 mL) olive oil in a large skillet over high heat. Dump the mushrooms into the oil and let a crust develop. Add the shallots and toss. Cook the mushrooms until softened. Remove from heat and add the brown butter mixture. Reserve for plating.

BOK CHOY Add the sesame and vegetable oils to a skillet over high heat. Add the halved bok choy, cut side down, to the skillet and cook for 1 minute. Add the garlic, ginger, salt, and water. Cover with a lid, reduce heat to medium, and allow to steam for 2 to 3 minutes until tender.

Assembly

Add the rice to 4 bowls. Top rice with the mushrooms and bok choy and drizzle some of the lemon soy butter from the mushroom pan equally into each bowl. Place the salmon on top and garnish with sesame seeds. Enjoy!

FISH TIP

Cooking salmon for a big crowd can be really relaxing. When cooking for lots of people, I like to cook whole sides of salmon. It takes longer in the oven to cook, which allows you time to work on other things. When the salmon is cooked, it's easy to portion with a spatula and serve right into your bowl.

This is in the late 80's—we had just caught a bunch of coho on the Sunshine Coast and were showing off our catch. I'm with my dad and uncle Wayne.

FISHERMAN'S PIE

with Puff Pastry "Barnacles"

SERVES 4 TO 6

10 oz (285 g) haddock, cut into large cubes

½ lb (250 g) salmon, cut into large cubes

1 uncooked lobster tail (about 2 oz/60 g), cut into large cubes

1 whole egg + 1 yolk, lightly beaten

2 puff pastry sheets, thawed

POACHING LIQUID

2 cups (500 mL) milk

Pinch of nutmeg

3 sprigs thyme

½ tsp (2.5 mL) diced garlic

¼ tsp (1 mL) salt

PIE FILLING

2 Tbsp (30 mL) vegetable oil

1 cup (250 mL) diced onion

1 tsp (5 mL) diced garlic

1 cup (250 mL) chopped celery

2 Tbsp (30 mL) unsalted butter

2 Tbsp (30 mL) all-purpose flour

⅓ cup (80 mL) fish stock

½ tsp (2.5 mL) Worcestershire sauce

Salt, to taste

Breaking through this crispy puff pastry sounds like the crackle of dry wood on a campfire, followed by the hypnotizing aroma of tarragon and seafood. It will overwhelm all of your senses, not just your taste buds.

It's very satisfying when you can serve something in the same vessel you cooked it in. All you need is a stack of small plates, your favourite salad, and a glass of wine.

"Well, here I am baby! What are your other two wishes?"

Method

POACHING LIQUID Warm the milk, nutmeg, thyme, garlic, and salt in a pot over medium-low heat. Add the haddock and salmon cubes and poach for 2 to 3 minutes.

PIE FILLING Preheat oven to 375°F (190°C).

Heat 2 Tbsp (30 mL) vegetable oil in a skillet over medium-high heat. Add the onion and sweat for a minute. Add the garlic and celery and cook for another minute. Add the butter and let it melt, then add the flour and mix to create a roux. Add half the poaching liquid (holding back the fish) and whisk until you have a thick sauce; whisk in the remaining poaching liquid. Once thick, add the fish stock and stir to combine.

Let thicken one more time then fold in the fish. Season with Worcestershire sauce and salt to taste.

Assembly

Pour the pie filling mixture into a 10- × 13-inch (25 × 33 cm) baking dish. Make an egg wash with the whole egg and extra yolk and brush it on the outside edges of the pastry sheet that will contact the baking dish. Cover the pie with the 2 sheets of puff pastry, sealing the edges around the dish. (If you have excess pastry you can add fun decorative pastry shapes.) Brush the top with egg wash and bake in the oven for 35 to 45 minutes, until the pastry is golden brown.

. . . recipe continued

FISH TIP

Poaching fish in milk has two huge advantages, the first being that the fish becomes very tender while cooking in the milk fat at a low temperature. The other is flavour. Steep the milk with lots of aromatics and let the milk become really flavourful before you add the fish. Once it's cooked, you are left with super tender fish and an incredibly well-seasoned "broth" for a sauce or fish pie.

SAN FRANCISCO CIOPPINO

with Mussels / Clams / Jumbo Shrimp / Sole

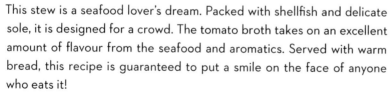

This stew is a seafood lover's dream. Packed with shellfish and delicate sole, it is designed for a crowd. The tomato broth takes on an excellent amount of flavour from the seafood and aromatics. Served with warm bread, this recipe is guaranteed to put a smile on the face of anyone who eats it!

The best way to serve this Bay Area fish stew is with deep bowls and a big ladle. I put the Dutch oven in the middle of the table and serve it family style.

"And as my life flashed before my eyes, all I remembered was that seafood stew. It was glorious."

Method

Wash and clean the mussels and remove any beards.

Heat 1 Tbsp (15 mL) vegetable oil in a frying pan over medium-high heat and add the fennel seeds; toast for 1 minute. Add the onion and garlic and sweat for 30 seconds. Add the fennel, celery, carrots, and cook for 1 minute. Deglaze the pan with white wine and reduce by half.

Add the tomato purée, fish stock, salt, and pepper and stir to combine. Add the potatoes and chili flakes and cook until the potatoes are 80% cooked.

Add the mussels, clams, and shrimp and cover with a lid. Allow to steam for 3 minutes. Stir in the butter and parsley. Roll up the sole and place it in the stew. Cover the pot, turn the burner off, and remove from heat. Allow to sit for 3 minutes. Serve warm with your favourite crusty bread.

. . . recipe continued

SERVES 4 TO 6

1 lb (450 g) mussels

1 lb (450 g) clams

12 shrimp, peeled and deveined (see Fish Tip, page 201)

4 fillets of sole

Crusty bread, for serving

CIOPPINO

1 Tbsp (15 mL) vegetable oil

½ tsp (2.5 mL) fennel seeds

½ cup (125 mL) diced onion

1 Tbsp (15 mL) diced garlic

2 cups (500 mL) chopped fennel

½ cup (125 mL) chopped celery

½ cup (125 mL) diced carrots

½ cup (125 mL) white wine

3 cups (750 mL) tomato purée

3 cups (750 mL) fish stock

1 tsp (5 mL) salt

1 tsp (5 mL) pepper

2 cups (500 mL) diced potatoes

¼ tsp (1 mL) chili flakes

2 Tbsp (30 mL) unsalted butter

2 Tbsp (30 mL) chopped parsley

FISH TIP

Let's talk fish stock! It's so great to have around. Like chicken stock or beef stock, it gives that extra added depth that restaurant cooking has. Use stock in place of water in most recipes and it will up your game. It's so simple, but so effective! You can find fish stock at the store or make it yourself and freeze it; clam nectar is also a great alternative.

SEAFOOD-STUFFED JUMBO SHELLS

with Puttanesca Sauce / Braised Spinach /
Crab and Ricotta Stuffing / Garlic Shrimp

SERVES 4 TO 6

3 cups (750 mL) Dungeness crab meat

12 large butterflied shrimp, peeled and deveined (see Fish Tip, page 201)

20 jumbo pasta shells

Olive oil, for drizzling over the shells

Parmesan cheese, to taste

PUTTANESCA SAUCE

1 Tbsp (15 mL) olive oil

⅓ cup (80 mL) diced onion

1 tsp (5 mL) minced garlic

2 tsp (10 mL) chopped capers

⅓ cup (80 mL) pitted and chopped Kalamata olives

⅓ cup (80 mL) chopped sun-dried tomatoes

1 cup (250 mL) red wine

1 tsp (5 mL) sugar

1½ cups (375 mL) tomato purée

¼ tsp (1 mL) salt

¼ tsp (1 mL) pepper

Pinch of chili flakes

½ cup (125 mL) water

BRAISED SPINACH

1 Tbsp (15 mL) vegetable oil

4 cups (1 L) spinach

Salt, to taste

Pepper, to taste

. . . ingredients continued

Stuffed seafood shells with a tangy sauce of Italian tomatoes, roasted peppers, sun-dried tomatoes, olives, and salty anchovies? Yes, please! This pasta rocks, and my favourite part is the pasta-to-seafood ratio. With creamy ricotta and braised spinach, do not count on leftovers.

My favourite cooking and plating vessel happen to be the same for this recipe: a nice, deep, oval-shaped porcelain casserole dish. It's perfect for cooking and serving—just add a serving spoon.

"Imagine opening your box of Cracker Jack and there's no popcorn, just 12 prizes."

Method

JUMBO PASTA SHELLS Bring a large pot of salted water to a hard boil and cook the pasta shells according to the package instructions. Remove the shells from the water and place on a baking tray. Drizzle with olive oil and cover with a damp towel until ready to stuff.

PUTTANESCA SAUCE Heat 1 Tbsp (15 mL) olive oil in a frying pan over medium-high heat. Sauté the onion and garlic for 30 seconds. Add the capers, olives, and sun-dried tomatoes and cook for 2 minutes. Deglaze the pan with the red wine and add the sugar. Reduce by half. Add the tomato purée and season with the salt, pepper, and chili flakes. Add the water and simmer over low heat until the sauce is thick enough to coat the back of a spoon. Keep warm over low heat.

BRAISED SPINACH Heat 1 Tbsp (15 mL) olive oil in a skillet over medium-high heat. Add the spinach and cook while turning several times to wilt. Season with the salt and pepper to taste and set aside.

CRAB AND RICOTTA STUFFING Mix the crab meat with the ricotta, pepper, and lemon zest until well combined. Put the mixture into a piping bag and cut a quarter-size hole in the end.

. . . recipe continued

PASTA SHELLS CONTINUED Preheat oven to 325°F (165°C).

Spread ½ cup (125 mL) of the puttanesca sauce on the bottom of a baking dish or baking tray with sides. Using the piping bag full of ricotta and crab, fill each pasta shell and place on top of the sauce. Stagger the braised spinach around the shells and top with any remaining sauce. Sprinkle the entire tray with Parmesan cheese and bake for 10 minutes.

GARLIC SHRIMP Melt the butter in a frying pan over high heat and add the butterflied shrimp and garlic. Cook until slightly pink and season with the salt. Remove from heat and add the shrimp to the hot baked pasta. Pour any butter left in the pan overtop. Serve hot and enjoy!

FISH TIP

When I'm looking for crab, I always buy fresh and local. I often use Dungeness crab, but it can be on the pricey side. An alternative is snow crab, which is equally sweet and delicious.

If you want a real bang for your buck, save the shells and make soup or sauce with them. The shells have unbelievable flavour and, with a few vegetables and seasonings, you can stretch your dollar and have some delicious dishes along the way.

CRAB AND RICOTTA STUFFING

3 cups (750 mL) ricotta cheese

½ tsp (2.5 mL) pepper

1 Tbsp (15 mL) lemon zest

GARLIC SHRIMP

1 Tbsp (15 mL) unsalted butter

1 tsp (5 mL) grated garlic

¼ tsp (1 mL) salt

SPECIAL EQUIPMENT

Piping bag

BBQ GLAZED BLACK COD PIZZA

with Hoisin Pizza Sauce / Chili Ginger Marmalade / Asian Greens

Fish on pizza? Yes, absolutely! This recipe is so exciting, I'm drooling right now just thinking about it. The best part is that the pizza crust is cooked with no topping on it to begin with. This allows you to get the pizza crust super crispy, and when you want to eat your pizza you can just simply add your toppings and the cooked fish and warm it up. The natural fattiness of the black cod goes so well with the Chinese BBQ sauce, Jack cheese, and an exhilarating chili ginger marmalade. This is such a fun way for the family to eat fish.

Pizza served on the platter or pie sheet it was cooked on is the only way to go. Have the plates and napkins on the table and it's go time.

"Twice a day I convince myself I am a bona fide genius."

Method

Preheat oven to 400°F (200°C).

Toss a bit of flour on your work surface. Roll out the pizza dough to fit your pizza stone or the back of a baking tray. Bake in the oven for 10 minutes or until lightly golden. Remove from the oven.

Season the black cod fillets with a pinch of five-spice powder and place on a parchment-lined baking sheet. Bake for 6 minutes.

HOISIN PIZZA SAUCE Combine all the hoisin pizza sauce ingredients in a bowl and mix well. Set aside.

CHILI GINGER MARMALADE Mix the ginger and green onion with the remaining chili ginger marmalade ingredients (or chop together in a mini food processor). Set aside.

ASIAN GREENS Toss the pea shoots and cilantro together with the vinegar, vegetable oil, sesame oil, and salt. Reserve for garnish.

PIZZA Paint the pizza dough with the hoisin pizza sauce. Flake the black cod fillets overtop and sprinkle with Jack cheese and chili ginger marmalade. Bake until the cheese is bubbly.

. . *recipe continued*

SERVES 4

1 ball of pizza dough

Two 4 oz (125 g) black cod fillets

Chinese five-spice powder

1 cup (250 mL) grated Jack cheese

HOISIN PIZZA SAUCE

1 Tbsp (15 mL) hoisin sauce

2 Tbsp (30 mL) BBQ sauce

½ tsp (2.5 mL) sugar

⅓ cup (80 mL) crushed tomatoes

2 tsp (10 mL) minced ginger

¼ tsp (1 mL) five-spice powder

CHILI GINGER MARMALADE

3 Tbsp (45 mL) chopped ginger

2 Tbsp (30 mL) chopped green onion

1 tsp (5 mL) sugar

3 Tbsp (45 mL) chili oil

¼ tsp (1 mL) salt

ASIAN GREENS

½ cup (125 mL) pea shoots

½ cup (125 mL) chopped cilantro

1 tsp (5 mL) rice wine vinegar

1 tsp (5 mL) vegetable oil

½ tsp (2.5 mL) sesame oil

Pinch of salt

GARNISH

Chili oil

Peanuts, crushed

. . . BBQ Glazed Black Cod Pizza (continued)

Assembly

Cut the pizza and garnish with the Asian greens. Drizzle with chili oil and crushed peanuts. Enjoy!

FISH TIP

There are two types of fish out there that are super similar: black cod and sablefish. I'm here to tell you that they are the same thing. Prized for their fat and super-rich buttery texture, these choices hold the #1 spot for my all-time favourite fish.

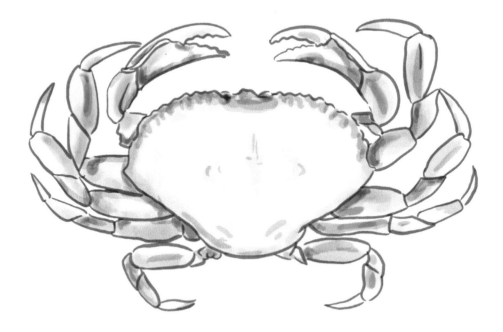

PIRI PIRI-MARINATED COD FILLETS

with Salsa Verde / Orzo Succotash

SERVES 4 TO 6

1 side of cod

PIRI PIRI MARINADE

1 Tbsp (15 mL) diced ginger

1 Tbsp (15 mL) crushed garlic

⅓ cup (80 mL) hot sauce

½ tsp (2.5 mL) smoked paprika

1 Tbsp (15 mL) lemon juice

½ cup + 1 Tbsp (140 mL) vegetable oil

SALSA VERDE

3 cups (750 mL) cilantro

1 tsp (5 mL) chopped garlic

¼ cup (60 mL) olive oil

¼ tsp (1 mL) chili flakes

1 Tbsp (15 mL) lemon juice

1 cup (250 mL) parsley

¼ tsp (1 mL) salt

ORZO SUCCOTASH

1 cup (250 mL) orzo pasta

1 Tbsp (15 mL) vegetable oil

⅓ cup (80 mL) diced onion

1 Tbsp (15 mL) crushed garlic

1½ cups (375 mL) diced zucchini

½ cup (125 mL) corn

1 cup (250 mL) seeded and diced
Roma tomatoes

1 Tbsp (15 mL) unsalted butter

½ tsp (2.5 mL) lemon juice

1½ cups (375 mL) chopped parsley

¼ tsp (1 mL) salt

¼ tsp (1 mL) pepper

Orzo pasta is so great for a meal in a hurry. In this recipe it cooks up fast and takes on a ton of flavour from the vegetables, butter, and herbs. The piri piri marinade is vibrant, fresh, and can be made ahead of time. The salsa verde packs a punch and brings the whole meal together. With little effort, this family meal can be on the table in no time.

This is the perfect family style meal. You can serve the orzo separately and leave the fish dancing in its sauce, making each person the master of their own dinner destiny, or you can plate them together for a colourful and delicious extravaganza.

"Brace yourself for high fives and praise. You are now the master of dinner."

Method

PIRI PIRI MARINADE Combine all the piri piri marinade ingredients in a bowl and mix well. Place the cod in a sealable bag and pour the marinade overtop. Seal the bag and store in the fridge for 1 to 2 hours.

SALSA VERDE Combine all the salsa verde ingredients in a small food processor and blitz to combine. Pour into a bowl and cover until ready to use.

ORZO SUCCOTASH Cook the orzo pasta according to the package instructions and reserve.

Heat 1 Tbsp (15 mL) vegetable oil in a frying pan over high heat and add the onion and garlic. Sauté for 1 minute, then add the zucchini and cook for another minute. Add the corn and tomatoes and cook for 1 minute more. Add the cooked orzo pasta, butter, lemon juice, parsley, salt, and pepper. Keep warm.

COD Preheat oven to 400°F (200°C).

Remove the cod from the marinade and place it on a parchment-lined baking sheet; bake for 8 to 10 minutes. The internal temperature of the fish should reach 145°F (63°C) and be tender and flaky in the middle.

Assembly

Serve the marinated cod warm with small spoonfuls of salsa verde on top and the orzo succotash on the side.

. . . recipe continued

FISH TIP

Marinating fish is such a good way to retain its moisture and add lots of flavour. Use a glass bowl or Pyrex dish and cover with a towel to avoid using single-use plastics. This works great for flavour engagement, and clean-up is simple. Plus, the planet is happier for it. Clean kitchen, tasty dinner, happy home.

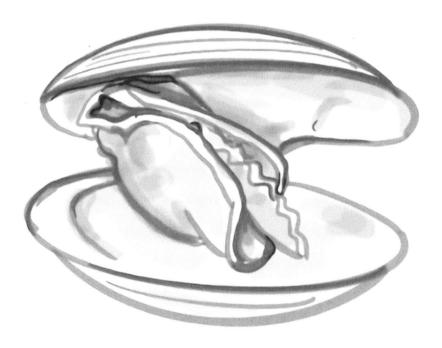

SMOKY TOMATO RISOTTO
with Ling Cod / Mussels / Clams / Shrimp

Seafood risotto has made an appearance throughout my culinary career. It's one of those dishes that has just stuck. It packs a ton of seafood, and the slightly spicy chorizo gives the right amount of zing. Finished with butter and cheese, this risotto will be mother tested and kid approved.

This is another one-pot dish that is perfect for the whole family. Whether you serve it family style in the pot you cooked it in or plate it individually, it will feed the whole gang. It's the kind of comforting meal that really sticks to your ribs.

"Every time Janice heats up her leftovers in the office microwave, it smells like a #%$! restaurant!"

Method

RISOTTO Warm the vegetable stock and saffron in a pot over medium heat.

Heat 2 Tbsp (30 mL) olive oil in a heavy-bottomed pot over medium heat. Add 1 Tbsp (15 mL) diced onion and 1 tsp (5 mL) garlic and sauté for 1 minute. Add the Arborio rice and toast for 60 seconds while stirring. Add ½ cup (125 mL) stock to the rice and stir. Cook while stirring until the stock is mostly absorbed. Continue adding the warm stock to the rice, ½ cup (125 mL) at a time while stirring, allowing the stock to be mostly absorbed into the rice before adding the next scoop. Continue until the stock is gone and the rice has become creamy. Season the risotto with salt and pepper to taste, remove from heat, and set aside.

LING COD Preheat oven to 400°F (200°C).

Line a baking sheet with parchment paper. Place the cod on the parchment and season with salt and pepper. Cook in the oven for 3 to 4 minutes.

RISOTTO CONTINUED Heat 1 Tbsp (15 mL) vegetable oil in a large pot over medium-high heat. Add the remaining onion and garlic and the sliced chorizo; sauté for 1 minute until they begin to soften. Add the crushed tomatoes, water, and paprika and mix well. Add the cooked risotto and the raw mussels, clams, and shrimp and stir to combine. Cover with a lid and cook for 4 minutes over medium heat.

. . . recipe continued

SERVES 4 TO 6

½ lb (250 g) ling cod, cut into chunks

1 lb (450 g) mussels

½ lb (250 g) clams

12 large shrimp, peeled and deveined (see Fish Tip, page 201)

Salt, to taste

Pepper, to taste

RISOTTO

4 cups (1 L) vegetable stock

¼ tsp (1 mL) saffron

2 Tbsp (30 mL) olive oil

½ cup + 1 Tbsp (140 mL) diced onion, divided

2 tsp (10 mL) diced garlic, divided

1 cup (250 mL) Arborio rice

Salt, to taste

Pepper, to taste

1 Tbsp (15 mL) vegetable oil

2 links chorizo dried sausage, sliced into coins

1 cup (250 mL) crushed tomatoes

1½ cups (375 mL) water

1 tsp (5 mL) smoked paprika

¼ cup (60 mL) unsalted butter

¼ cup (60 mL) grated Parmesan cheese

¼ cup (60 mL) chopped cilantro

GARNISH

Cilantro, chopped

Remove the lid. Discard any mussels that didn't open.

Stir in the butter, Parmesan cheese, and cilantro, and top with the cooked ling cod. Season with ¼ tsp (1 mL) each salt and pepper.

Serve warm and enjoy!

FISH TIP

Ling cod is a perfect fish when it comes to sustainability. It has an amazing texture and can grow to upwards of 80 lb (36 kg). This means the loins can be quite thick, making it great for cooking. The thicker the fish, the easier to cook, and I find it tends to be much juicier.

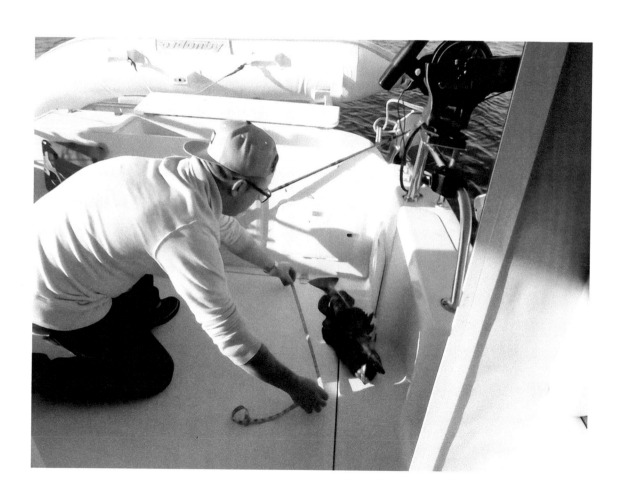

HAWAIIAN FAMILY DINNER

with Halibut Steaks / BBQ Pork Rice / Tropical Salsa

2 large halibut steaks
(about 8 oz/230 g each)

4 oz (125 g) BBQ pork, diced
(available premade at Asian
markets, or use your favourite)

Cooking spray (or vegetable oil)

Salt, to taste

Pepper, to taste

BBQ PORK RICE

1 cup (250 mL) uncooked
jasmine rice

½ cup (125 mL) coconut milk

¼ tsp (1 mL) lime juice

¼ tsp (1 mL) salt

¼ tsp (1 mL) sugar

2 Tbsp (30 mL) unsalted butter

2 Tbsp (30 mL) chopped cilantro

TROPICAL SALSA

1 cup (250 mL) finely diced papaya

1 cup (250 mL) diced mango

½ cup (125 mL) finely diced
red onion

½ cup (125 mL) chopped cilantro

1 tsp (5 mL) honey

1 tsp (5 mL) lime juice

½ cup (125 mL) seeded and diced
fresh tomato

One of the things I love about Hawaiian food is that it's a feast in so many ways—the food is amazing, it's visually intoxicating and fresh, and it feels like a party every time you sit down, making everyone at the table smile. This halibut steak dinner is just that—a party of delicious food that will make you want to dance. The salty and sweet BBQ pork rice will stick to your ribs, and the thick-cut halibut is fresh and simple, letting the tropical salsa bring it to life.

Hawaii is my second home, and for a meal like this, I can't help getting right into it. I like to use coconuts for bowls. Small bamboo steamers are cheap and great for steaming, but also as decor. Let your imagination take you to the luau and have fun with it. Your family will thank you for the escape.

Method

BBQ PORK RICE Cook the rice according to package instructions, replacing ½ cup (125 mL) water with ½ cup (125 mL) coconut milk and adding the lime juice, salt, sugar, and diced BBQ pork.

Once cooked, let stand for 10 minutes. Add the butter and fluff the rice. Add the cilantro and stir it in just before serving.

TROPICAL SALSA Place the diced fruit in a bowl. Add the remaining tropical salsa ingredients and toss to coat. Cover and refrigerate until ready to serve.

HALIBUT Spray the halibut with cooking spray (or brush with oil) and season with salt and pepper. Grill over high heat on the barbecue or in a grill pan for 4 minutes per side, until the fish is tender and cooked all the way through.

Assembly

I like to plate this feast luau style. I love to serve the fried rice in little steam pots. I plate everything and leave the fish for last. It's super fun and playful to serve the salsa in a hollowed-out half-pineapple.

. . . recipe continued

FISH TIP

When grilling fish, I always spray the fish with a good quality cooking spray first. This will make the fish absolutely not stick when it hits the grill. It's the best pregrill technique I have ever used when grilling fish of any kind.

ALMOND-CRUSTED TROUT

with Gruyère Galette / Grape Beurre Blanc

The first time I had a grape beurre blanc I was in Hawaii and I nearly fell off my chair, it was that good. I later learned that it is a classic French sauce, and there is no other nation that knows the art of how to use butter in food better than the French. The galette is salty and chewy and decadent, and with this nut-crusted trout, it's a marriage made in heaven.

This is a thin fish, and I like to stack it high and let the butter sauce drip and fall all around so it starts a riot at the table.

Method

GRUYÈRE GALETTE Preheat oven to 375°F (190°C).

Peel the potatoes and, using a mandoline, slice them into paper-thin rounds. Heat 2 Tbsp (30 mL) clarified butter in a 9-inch (23 cm) cast iron skillet over medium-high heat; place the potatoes around the base of the pan, overlapping the edges of each slice until the entire base of the pan is covered. Season with salt and pepper. Paint with the remaining clarified butter and cover with another layer of potatoes. Repeat until all the potato slices are used. Top with Gruyère cheese.

Bake in the oven for 30 minutes, until the potatoes on the bottom are crispy and the cheese is bubbling. Reserve and keep warm.

Reduce oven temperature to 245°F (120°C) for the trout.

GRAPE BEURRE BLANC Combine the water, shallots, lemon juice, and garlic in a frying pan over medium heat. Add a cube of cold butter to the pan and swirl. As it melts, add another cube of butter and continue swirling the pan and adding butter until all the butter has melted and the sauce has thickened. Add the grapes, parsley, and a pinch of salt to finish. Reserve and keep warm.

ALMOND-CRUSTED TROUT Place the almonds on a parchment-lined baking tray and bake in the preheated oven for 30 minutes. Remove and cool slightly.

Toss the toasted almonds into a food processor and give them a blitz. (You can also crush them with a rolling pin.) Spread them out on a flat plate and press each trout fillet into the almonds. Heat 2 Tbsp (30 mL) vegetable oil in a frying pan over medium-high heat. Add the almond-crusted trout and cook for 1 to 2 minutes per side.

. . . recipe continued

SERVES 4 TO 6

1 cup (250 mL) sliced almonds

Two 1 lb (450 g) whole lake trouts, filleted into 8 skinless portions

2 Tbsp (30 mL) vegetable oil

GRUYÈRE GALETTE

4 to 5 large russet potatoes

⅓ cup (80 mL) clarified butter, divided

¼ tsp (1 mL) salt

¼ tsp (1 mL) pepper

½ cup (125 mL) grated Gruyère cheese

GRAPE BEURRE BLANC

2 tsp (10 mL) water

2 Tbsp (30 mL) finely diced shallots

2 tsp (10 mL) lemon juice

½ tsp (2.5 mL) grated garlic

½ cup (125 mL) cubed unsalted butter, chilled

¼ cup (60 mL) sliced green grapes

¼ cup (60 mL) chopped parsley

Pinch of salt

Assembly

Stack the almond-crusted trout fillets on a plate and drizzle with the grape beurre blanc. Fill a pitcher with the rest of the beurre blanc and let people pour onto their fish as they desire. Cut the Gruyère galette into wedges and serve warm. Enjoy!

FISH TIP

Lake trout are mild in flavour, delicate, and tender. They have less fat than salmon and a less-intense flavour. I like to buy whole lake trout and fillet them myself. If I see it at a small local fish-monger near a lake, I grab it every time.

The trick to filleting your own fish is in the knife. You want a flexible knife that can bend. Get the right knife and practice, and you will be filleting your own fish in no time.

ACKNOWLEDGMENTS

To my mother Linda Watts. They say that the drummer is the backbone of the band and I can honestly say you have been the backbone to my career and all my crazy ideas. We have had so many adventures attached to food and all of those have led up to so many great accomplishments, from a small cable show where you were the dishwasher, set designer, and producer, to helping me film and send in VHS tapes to the Food Network, driving me to cooking competitions, consoling me when I lost, and hugging me when I won. You have designed menus and proposals for me, we opened a restaurant what seems like a lifetime ago, we've had premiere parties for my debut on television and many more adventures that you and I laugh about with great pride. Well Mom, now we can add a cookbook. You have been there for the really hard times and always brought a huge smile to the really great times, your calm loving nature and ability to not break my spirit has been paramount to everything I have accomplished. If you take yourself out of this equation it would take 100 lifetimes to try and recreate the success I have had. Without you, Mom, it just doesn't work. I love you and thank you for being right by my side for this lifelong journey, and cheers to our first cookbook.

To my dad, this book would not have been possible without your love for the water and fishing. Passing that on to me and Travis defiantly shaped who I am today. I will pass on the things you have taught me about mother ocean and travelling on her safely and respectfully to my children. This book has a soul and you helped build that, the stories that are in this book have one common thread and that's you, Dad. I hope when you read this book you think of all of our crazy adventures on the boat and all the wonderful times we had as a family cooking, fishing, and laughing. You're my hero, Dad, and I thank you for being at the helm.

To my brother, Travis. WILSON I think we did it! I won the sibling lottery and I love ya man. You always bring a smile to my face whenever we see each other and I hope this book brings a smile to yours. I dedicated a chapter in this book to you Travis because I have the best bro in the world. Let's keep teaching our kids our love for food and how to catch fish. To my sister, Asza, I hope this book makes you proud. We have always bonded over food and I will always love your cooking questions. You're one of the best humans I know and I love that you and my wife are thicker than thieves.

To the team. First off, Kathy, this book is a dream come true and physically would not have been possible without you. Thank you from the bottom of my heart for everything you have put into this book, your time, your many contributions, and your insane drive to get this book on shelves. Of course, thanks to your family's time and your dear husband's coffee makers that were on overtime during development and photography. Thank you for letting us turn your home into a studio once again and, Craig, you are the man! Kathy I am so grateful to have you as a friend, partner, and mentor, you're just the best. So, Thank You. Mr. West, getting to know you and work with you has been one of the great joys in my life. Thank you for always making me feel like "I got this" and pumping me up. I know in years to come they will talk about West & Watts like they do Burton and Depp. Thanks for all of your hard work man. And cut! Steph, thank you for capturing these creations and for all the hard work you put into post-production, plus all the feedback Ian gave on the food you would take home to him, you guys rock. And to the best illustrator and artist in the game, Eimear, thank you for adding your incredible talents to this book. You have seamlessly captured my adventures using the perfect medium.

To my best friend, Rory Higdon. I never thought in a million years that meeting you as a fresh faced dishwasher all those years ago would lead to culinary domination, building a business together, and becoming great friends. What a wild ride it has been. Thanks for always having time for me and for always being willing to beat up an idea. I love creating food and concepts, but doing it with you is always better. Cheers Rory.

To the team at Whitecap. Thank you guys for believing in this book and helping us take it through the finish line. We are so proud of this cookbook and we thank you all for your time and dedication.

They say you save the best for last so . . . to my wife, Sophia. This book has been a constant in our life over the past year. The support you have given to me in order to work on this in the office for hours, days, and nights on end is truly incredible. Thank you for helping me filter my ideas and articulate them properly, you truly know my voice and if it wasn't for you going through this cookbook word for word it would not be where it is. Our first daughter was only three weeks old before I had to leave for a month and develop the recipes and complete photography. Sophia, you are the most selfless woman I know, you put everyone first and the qualities you have as a woman are extraordinary. I hope you look at this body of work and are proud of what we did together. Thank you will never be enough. I love you girls with all my heart and I know we will all sleep well once this book is printed. To my wife's family, aka the Lazazzera clan, thank you all for the continuous support, love you all.

Some of you might be thinking "what's this pic got to do with Spencer's food?" Well if you look past the adorable superman outfit that I loved you will see that I am watching a food tv show. This was the beginning of my love affair with food . . . and I'm obviously . . . super.

INDEX

lobster
about, 78, 93, 149, 172
"Big Catch" Seafood Chowder, 48
Creole Shellfish Bisque, 53
Drunken Lobster Noodles, 149
Fisherman's Pie, 216
Lobster Puffs, 90
Lobster Scotch Egg, 171
Shellfish Cassoulet, 187
Warm Lobster Potato Salad, 77
lump crab cake, 53

M

mahi mahi
about, 104
Mahi Mahi Banh Mi Submarine, 95
Jerk-Rubbed Mahi Mahi Tacos, 103
mangoes
avocado–mango salsa, 22
tropical salsa, 240
maple syrup
Wasabi–Maple Vinaigrette, 35
mayonnaise
chipotle remoulade, 103
curry mayo, 171
garlic butter aioli, 90
miracle mayo, 117
spicy Sriracha mayo, 22
wasabi sesame mayo, 111
whipped mayonnaise, 166
mignonette, rosé, 35
miso
Miso Honey–Glazed Salmon Rice Bowls, 213
Oven-Broiled Sweet Miso Oysters, 43

mortadella
Smoked Salmon, Salami, and Mortadella Muffuletta Sandwich, 120
mushrooms
Miso Honey–Glazed Salmon Rice Bowls, 213
shiitake mushroom vinaigrette, 72
Thai-Style Seafood "Bouillabaisse", 56
mussels
about, 169
Baked Mussels on the Half Shell, 30
San Francisco Cioppino, 221
Smoky Tomato Risotto, 237
Steamed P.E.I. Mussels, 166
Thai-Style Seafood "Bouillabaisse", 56

N

noodles. *See also* pasta
Drunken Lobster Noodles, 149
Pork & Shrimp Dan Dan Noodles, 130
nori
Crispy Fish and Chip Sushi Roll, 182
nuts
Almond-Crusted Trout, 245
Roasted Black Cod Pappardelle, 141

O

olives
Anchovy & Carmelized Onion Tart, 150
pickled pepper tapenade, 120

puttanesca sauce, 224
sun-dried tomato and tarragon vinaigrette, 77
onions
Anchovy & Carmelized Onion Tart, 150
Bay Scallop and Shrimp Quiche, 195
caramelized onion and anchovy spread, 90
orzo succotash, 232
oysters
Cornmeal Fried Popcorn Oysters, 38
Fresh Shucked Oysters, 35
Oven-Broiled Sweet Miso Oysters, 43
shucking, 36, 41

P

pancetta
Bay Scallop and Shrimp Quiche, 195
pancetta and Medjool date marmalade, 203
sage cream, 141
panko breadcrumbs
Crab Cake Sliders, 98
Dungeness Crab Fritters, 19
herbed breadcrumbs, 30
Lobster Scotch Egg, 171
Oven-Broiled Sweet Miso Oysters, 43
Pan-Fried Crispy Sole, 174
Panko-Crusted Halibut & Scallop "Chop" Burger, 117
Panko Herb-Crusted Side of Salmon, 208
parsley gremolata, 136

Spicy "Crunch Roll" Albacore
   Tuna Poke, 22

V

vegetable caponata, 144
vegetable confetti, 53

W

walleye
   Thai-Style Seafood "Bouilla-
      baisse", 56
wasabi–maple vinaigrette, 35
wasabi popcorn, 85
wasabi sesame mayo, 111
wraps
   Korean Chili-Marinated
      Salmon Lettuce Wraps, 106
   Sea Bass & Chickpea Falafel,
      112

X

XO tomato jam, 95

Y

yogurt
   garlic yogurt, 112
   lemon yogurt, 19

Z

zucchini
   Dungeness Crab Fritters, 19
   orzo succotash, 232
   vegetable caponata, 144